Copies available from :

The Secretary
The Medico-Chirurgical Society of Aberdeen,
Medical School, Foresterhill, Aberdeen AB25 2ZD

Telephone: (+44)(0)1224 552737
Fax: (+44)(0)1224 550637
Email: medchi.admin@abdn.ac.uk
Website: www.med-chi.co.uk

ISBN 0 902604 67 8

The Heritage of the Med-Chi

Aberdeen Medico-Chirurgical Society

A collection of the portraits and
medical artefacts in the possession of
the Medico-Chirurgical Society of Aberdeen
(founded 1789)

A Adam & J D Hutchison

Cartoon of Matthew Hay as
Medical Officer of Health for Aberdeen
battling against disease
(from *Bon Accord*, 12 December 1891)

FOREWORD

This book is not meant to be a history of the Medico-Chirurgical Society of Aberdeen. That story has already been told in the excellent books by J Scott Riddell and G P Milne, the latter produced to celebrate the bicentenary of the Society in 1989. It is certainly a story worth telling, as befits one of the oldest Medical Societies in the world. And as might be expected of such a venerable institution, there is a historical collection of portraits and medical artefacts that is of national importance. This book seeks to bring together, for the first time, an account of these treasures.

Many members of the Med-Chi will be unaware of the existence of this legacy, as it has always been one of the greatest regrets of the Society that it has never had adequate room or resource to display this collection in a way that it deserves. However that may be about to change. As we write this, in 2007, plans are well advanced for the *Matthew Hay Project*. The construction of this building on the Foresterhill site beside Aberdeen Royal Infirmary will bring together the teaching of anatomy and clinical skills for medical students and others under one roof. It is fitting that it should be linked to that great Aberdonian medical visionary, Matthew Hay, who was responsible for the establishment of the Joint Hospitals Scheme which shaped medical

services in Aberdeen over the past 70 years. In this, he was strongly supported by Sir Ashley Mackintosh and the Medico-Chirurgical Society, and the Lord Provost of Aberdeen, Sir Andrew Lewis. The Society passed a Resolution (10th March, 1920), while Ashley Mackintosh was President, which stated that this was: *"... a specially opportune time for the consideration of a common site of such extent as to provide for ... almost the whole hospital system of the City. It is felt that the advantages of the concentration of the hospitals on such a common site would be incalculable in the interests of patients, as well as of the training of Medical Students and Nurses ... (and) to transfer to the same site the University departments most closely associated with clinical work."* Matthew Hay was a marvellous health administrator and organiser, and his vision of a "State Health Service" undoubtedly influenced the creation of the NHS – *"It is coming, it is only a matter of time."* (1916).

The proceeds of this book will help towards the funding of that building – our aim is to create something of which Aberdeen can be really proud, and one of the best of its type anywhere in the world.

A Adam
J D Hutchison

"All these were honoured in their generations, and were the glory of their times"

Ecclesiasticus

Acknowledgements

We have made full use of the excellent books that have been written on the history of the Medico-Chirurgical Society by J Scott Riddell and G P Milne, and *The Aberdeen Doctors* by E H B Rodger.

We have quoted liberally from J Scott Riddell (President of the Medico-Chirurgical Society, 1921-22) with a (relatively) clear conscience, on the basis that his choice of words and expressions are set down with such obvious good humour and affection, that they could not be bettered. And, more practically, because the book has been out of print for the best part of a century and is unlikely to make a re-appearance.

Interestingly, both J Scott Riddell's and Ella Rodger's books started life as Presidential Addresses to the Society, the latter being that of her husband, James Rodger, who was President in 1886-87.

J Scott Riddell

Similarly, there were many useful pieces of information and anecdote to be found in *A Bicentennial History 1789-1989*, edited by George P Milne (President of the Medico-Chirurgical Society, 1978), including a list of some of the treasures of the Med-Chi contributed by Ronnie Cumming, which was very helpful.

The beautiful photographs displayed in this book have come from a variety of sources, but mostly from the Department of Medical Illustration at the University of Aberdeen, and many of them were taken expressly for this book by Steven Hay (Medical Photographer). We hope that this publication does justice to his work, which has been of the highest quality. Over and above that, the helpfulness and cheerfulness of himself and his colleagues have been greatly appreciated.

The manuscript has been typed by our own secretary, Ms Gill Earle, who has also made many helpful suggestions, with help from Mrs Gillian Marshall in the Department of Surgery.

The encouragement – and advice – from Members and Council have also been greatly appreciated.

CONTENTS

Frontispiece iv

Foreword v

Acknowledgements vi

Contents vii

List of illustrations ix

PORTRAITS 1

Sir James McGrigor 2

John Grant 6

Robert Harvey 8

George Kerr 10

James Moir 12

The Founders' Plaque 14

William Harvey 16

William Livingston 20

George French 22

John Stuart 24

Robert Jamieson 26

William Dyce 28

George Watt 30

David Hutcheon 32

Joseph Williamson 34

John C Ogilvie 36

Rev. William Laing 38

Sir John Struthers 40

Sir Alexander Ogston 44

Sir Patrick Manson 50

J J R Macleod 52

Matthew Hay 54

Sir Ashley W Mackintosh 58

Sir John Marnoch 60

David W Finlay 62

The Medico-Chirurgical Society members in 1908 64

J Patrick S Nicoll 66

Sir Alexander Grieg Anderson 68

Sir Dugald Baird 70

Robert D Lockhart 72

BUSTS AND STATUETTES 75

Francis Adams 76

Alexander Kilgour 78

Alexander Harvey 80

Sir James McGrigor 82

Charles Murray 83

MISCELLANEOUS TREASURES 84

The Painting of a Dissection 84

Anatomical Drawings of Alberto Morrocco 86

The Hogarth Cartoon 88

The Chalmers Cartoon 89

The Etching of Hippocrates 90

The Death Mask of Napoleon 91

The Engraved Plate of the Society 94

The Seal of the Society 95

The Presidential Medallion 96

The Presidential Gown 97

The Ashley Mackintosh Golf Cup 98

The Silver Candlesticks 99

Hugo Rheinhold's *'Monkey contemplating a human skull'*	100
Silver Medal in the Practice of Medicine	102
The Keith Gold Medal	103
The Shepherd Memorial Gold Medal	104
The Cigarette Card Album	105
Dr Esslemont's CBE	106
Medical Women's Federation Medallion	107
The Grandfather Clock	108
The Lectern	109
The Ballot Boxes	110
The McGrigor Centenary Plaque	111
The War Memorial Plaque	112
The King Street Hall	114
The Subscription List	116
The Foresterhill Building	117
The Plane Tree	120
The Presidential Chair	121
The Member's Chairs	122
The Junior Members' President's Chair	123
The Kayak	124
The Library	126
The Students' Notes	127
Minute Books	128
Certificate awarded to Junior Members of the Society	132
Certificate awarded to the winner of the Strachan Bursary	133
The Med-Chi Student Elective Bursaries and the Adam Quaich	133
The McGrigor Archives	134
The Royal Letters and Telegrams	136
Joseph Black's Book on the Discovery of Carbon Dioxide	137
Dr Kilgour's Letter	138
The Apprenticeship Agreement	140
The Midwifery Certificate	142
Set of Surgical Instruments	144
The Collection of Stethoscopes	146
The Resuscitation Set	148
The Bleeding and Cupping Set	150
Tray of Chinese Instruments	152
Box of Surgical Instruments	153
The Society and the Medical School	154
The Annual Founders' Dinner	156
The Naughton Dunn Fund	160
MISSING TREASURES	162
William Stephenson	162
William Stirling	163
John A MacWilliam	164
David J Hamilton	165
John Theodore Cash	166
David Rorie	168
Sir Alastair Currie	171
Hans W Kosterlitz	172
John R Mallard	173
Endpiece: letter from HRH Queen Elizabeth, the Queen Mother on the 250th Anniversary of ARI	174
Index	177

LIST OF ILLUSTRATIONS

The Emblem of the Medico-Chirurgical Society of Aberdeen	iii
Frontispiece: Cartoon of Matthew Hay battling against disease	iv
J Scott Riddell	vi
Sir James McGrigor	3
Jamie McGrigor MSP	4
McGrigor's Obelisk	5
John Grant	7
Plaque in Belmont Street where Alexander Gordon lived	8
Alexander Gordon's *Treatise on the Epidemic Puerperal Fever*	8
Robert Harvey	9
Mortsafes in Banchory and Skene churchyards	10
Watchtower in Banchory churchyard	10
George Kerr	11
James Moir	13
The Founders' Plaque	15
William Harvey	17
Plaque to commemorate visit of William Harvey to Aberdeen	18
Extract from Town Council Minutes (1641)	19
Lord Byron	20
William Livingston	21
George French	23
John Stuart	25
Robert Jamieson	27
William Dyce	29
George Watt	31
David Hutcheon *by William Dyce*	32
David Hutcheon *by James Giles*	33
Extract from the Minute Book (1840) in Williamson's writing	34
Joseph Williamson	35
John Ogilvie	37
Rev William Laing	39
Professor Sir John Struthers (engraving)	41
Professor Sir John Struthers (portrait)	42
Cartoon of Professor Struthers as the Rag-and-Bone Man	42
Photograph of the crocodile	43
Professor Sir Alexander Ogston	45
Drawing of a bajan of Marischal College	46
Signed photograph of Professor Alexander Ogston	46
Photographs of an operation in Aberdeen using Ogston's spray	47
Ogston's spray	48
Microscope from Professor Ogston's Department	48
Aberdeen Royal Infirmary at Woolmanhill (1930)	49
Ward in Aberdeen Royal Infirmary at Woolmanhill	49
Operating Theatre in Aberdeen Royal Infirmary at Woolmanhill	49
Professor Sir Patrick Manson (portrait from The London School of Hygiene and Tropical Medicine)	50
Professor Sir Patrick Manson	51
Photograph of Professor J J R Macleod	52

Professor Macleod's Nobel Prize Medal	52	Charles Murray (bust)	83
Professor J J R Macleod	53	The Painting of a Dissection	85
Photograph of Professor Hay	54	Anatomical Drawings of Alberto Morrocco	86
Professor Matthew Hay (engraving)	55	The Hogarth Cartoon	88
Portrait of Professor Hay	56	The Chalmers Cartoon	89
Aberdeen Royal Infirmary through the years	57	The Etching of Hippocrates	90
		The Death Mask of Napoleon	91
Professor Sir Ashley Mackintosh	59	Report of the *post mortem* examination of Napoleon Bonaparte	92
Professor Sir John Marnoch	61	The Engraved Plate of the Society	94
Professor David Finlay	63		
The Medico-Chirurgical Society members in 1908 (key to montage)	64	The Seal of the Society	95
		The Presidential Medallion	96
The Medico-Chirurgical Society members in 1908	65	The Presidential Gown	97
		The Ashley Mackintosh Golf Cup	98
Dr Patrick Nicoll	67	The Silver Candlesticks	99
Sir Alexander Grieg Anderson (etching)	69	Hugo Rheinhold's *'Monkey contemplating a human skull'*	101
Photograph of Professor Baird	70	Silver Medal in the Practice of Medicine	102
Professor Sir Dugald Baird	71		
Professor R D Lockhart	73	The Keith Gold Medal	103
Professor R D Lockhart with his rhododendrons	74	Bladder stones	103
		Frontpiece of *First-Aid* book	104
Professor Lockhart's mother, Elizabeth	74	Surgeon Major Peter Shepherd	104
		The Cigarette Card Album	105
Francis Adams	75	Dr Mary Esslemont	106
Sir James McGrigor	75	Dr Esslemont's CBE	106
Photograph of Dr Francis Adams	76	Medical Women's Federation Medallion	107
Francis Adams (bust)	77		
Portrait of Dr Alexander Kilgour	78	The Grandfather Clock	108
Alexander Kilgour (bust)	79	The Lectern	109
Alexander Harvey (bust)	81	The Ballot Boxes	110
Statue of Sir James McGrigor in Millbank, London	82	The McGrigor Centenary Plaque	111
Sir James McGrigor (statue)	82	The War Memorial Plaque	113

Photographs of those named 113

The Meeting Hall in the King St building 114

The King Street Hall 115

The Subscription List 116

The Foresterhill Building 117

The Hall in the Med-Chi Building 118

The Council Chamber in the Med-Chi Building 119

The Plane Tree and plaque 120

The Presidential Chair 121

A Member's Chair 122

The Junior Members' President's Chair 123

Professor William Pirrie 124

Drawing of Eenoolooapik 125

The Kayak 125

The Library in the King Street Hall 126

The Students' Notes 127

Frontispiece of the first Minute Book 128

Extract from the Minute of 15th October 1790 128

Minutes of topics debated 1789-90 129

Regulations of the Society in the first Minute Book (1789) 130

Certificate awarded to Junior Members of the Society 132

Certificate awarded to the winner of the Strachan Bursary 133

The Adam Quaich 133

Letter from Sir James McGrigor 135

The Royal Letters and Telegrams 136

Joseph Black's Book on the Discovery of Carbon Dioxide 137

Dr Kilgour's Letter 139

The Apprenticeship Agreement 140

The Midwifery Certificate 143

Set of Surgical Instruments 145

The Collection of Stethoscopes 147

The Resuscitation Set 149

The Bleeding and Cupping Set 150

Tray of Chinese Instruments 152

Box of Surgical Instruments 153

Bishop Elphinstone 154

Extract from the *Aberdeen Lancet* (1831) 155

Copy of article from the *Shrewsbury Gazette* (1888) 155

Dinner Bill for Annual Dinner 1838 156

Front cover of Programme for the Centenary Founders' Dinner 1889 156

Dinner and Drinks Bills for Annual Dinner 1898 157

Extract from Minute Book relating to the Dinner 1902 158

Front covers of Programmes for the Annual Founders' Dinners 1906 & 1936 158

Front covers of the programmes for the Annual Founders' Dinners 1972, 1977, 1983 & 2006 159

The Widows' Fund Chest 160

The formation of the British Orthopaedic Association 1918 160

Naughton Dunn 161

Professor William Stephenson 162

Professor William Stirling 163

Cartoon of Professor Stirling 163

Professor John A MacWilliam 164

Professor David J Hamilton 165

Cartoon of Professor Cash	166
Professor J Theodore Cash	166
Professor Cash's collection of chemicals	167
Cartoon of Dr David Rorie	168
Dr David Rorie in uniform	169
Dr David Rorie	169
The Lum Hat	170
Professor Sir Alastair Currie	171
Professor Hans W Kosterlitz	172
The first whole body MRI scanner	173
Professor John R Mallard	173
Endpiece: HRH Queen Elizabeth, the Queen Mother	174
Letter from HRH Queen Elizabeth, the Queen Mother on the 250th Anniversary of ARI	175

PORTRAITS

The Society has an impressive collection of portraits of famous Aberdeen doctors from the past three centuries. These include Sir James McGrigor, several of the Founders of the Society, many of the great figures in medicine who have graced the Aberdonian stage, and also a portrait of *"the Great Harvey"*, possibly the single most valuable item in the collection. Many of the individuals whose portraits are reproduced here have been illustrious Presidents of our Society.

There are portraits by several famous artists, many with a North East of Scotland connection. These include:

James Giles, RSA (1801-1870) with paintings of *James Moir, George Watt, Joseph Williamson, John Ogilvie, Rev William Laing,* and probably *The Painting of a Dissection.*

John Moir (1741-1818) with portraits of *William Livingston, John Stuart* and *George French.*

William Dyce, RA (1806-1864) with portraits of his father, *William Dyce,* and the Society's lawyer, *David Hutcheon.* The *Painters' Window* in St Machar's Cathedral in Aberdeen is a memorial to three great Aberdonian artists: George Jamesone (*"the Scottish van Dyck"*), William Dyce and John Phillip (*"Phillip of Spain"*).

George Fiddes Watt, RSA (1873-1960) with the dominating portrait of the Society's Hall, that of *Sir Alexander Ogston.*

John Bulloch Souter (1890-1972) with a splendid portrait of *Sir Ashley Mackintosh,* and also *Patrick Nicoll.*

Alberto Morrocco, RSA (1917-1998) with portraits of *Sir Dugald Baird* and *Professor Lockhart's Mother.*

There are also outstanding works by Sir George Reid, RA (1841-1913 - *Professor Sir John Struthers* and *Robert Jamieson*), and Andrew Geddes (1783-1844 - *Sir James McGrigor,* the other large portrait in the Society's Hall).

The Founders

Sir James McGrigor, Bart, KCB, MA, MD, FRCP Edinburgh, London & Dublin, FRS London & Edinburgh, LLD (1771–1858).

"The Father of the Med-Chi and of the Army Medical Services"
(President of the Society, 1789)

James McGrigor was the son of an Aberdeen merchant and was a prize-winning scholar at the Grammar School. He attended Aberdeen Royal Infirmary as an apprentice and, to further his education, he went to Edinburgh for one year. On his return to Aberdeen, he founded the Medical Society with eleven other students to compensate for the lack of university education. At that time, the Universities of King's and Marischal in Aberdeen each had a Professor of Medicine, but they did not teach. The Medical Society was a self-help organisation, and the students held meetings, dissected dogs and invited lecturers. Gradually the medical profession in Aberdeen became involved, and the Society became a graduate as well as an undergraduate body. McGrigor was the driving force behind the Society and was its life-long supporter. It was he who proposed that the Society build its own meeting place, and he was prominent in fund-raising for this project. This building was opened in King Street in 1820. It was erected to the plans of Archibald Simpson, a well-known Aberdeen architect who also designed the rebuilt Aberdeen Royal Infirmary and the rebuilt Marischal College, both in 1840. The building cost over £3,000.

Sir James McGrigor joined the Army Medical Services as a regimental surgeon in 1794. He may well have been influenced early on in his medical studies by one of the senior students at the Infirmary, who had obtained an appointment as an Assistant Surgeon to a regiment. This young man immediately exchanged his round bonnet for a smart cocked hat with a cockade, and no doubt struck a handsome figure as the students gathered for the daily teaching ward rounds.

McGrigor was a natural leader and, because of his efficiency and attention to detail, he was rapidly promoted. In 1811, he was put in charge of the medical services on the Peninsula; these he transformed into an efficient organisation by improved care of the wounded and especially by a huge reduction in the rate of sickness. He was the first British Medical Officer to receive an official citation for the excellence of his work. The Duke of Wellington called him "Mac" and characterised him as *"one of the most industrious, able and successful public servants I have ever met with"*. After the Peninsular War, he was appointed Director of the Army Medical Department, a post which he held until he retired at the age of 80. When he was 75, he requested that he be allowed to retire, but the Commander in Chief of the Forces replied, *"No, no, McGrigor, there is plenty work left in you yet"*. He received many honours at home and abroad and was three times Rector of Marischal College. In 1860, a tall, red granite obelisk was erected in his memory in the quadrangle of Marischal College. In 1906, it was removed to its present site in Duthie Park.

In 1847, he sent, with a covering letter, approximately sixty volumes of the records of his army medical service from 1794 until the end of the Peninsular War in 1814. These records are amongst the most treasured possessions of the Society and are a valuable source of army medical history.

Sir James McGrigor (1771–1858)

McGrigor's links with the Society are all the more remarkable, given the response to his first address to the Society on *the History, Causes and Cure of Pleurisy*. This is reviewed in the Minute Book as follows: *"The exordium and conclusions of Mr McGrigor's discourse were very pathetic. If the author had done it justice by a good delivery it might possibly have brought the tears from our eyes."* One wonders whether, in the spirit of young men down the ages, this wasn't written with the tongue firmly in the cheek. Indeed, one of the Regulations (Minute Book 1, 1789) was: *"That no member commit any indecency during the meeting or in any way attempt to discourage the speaker or put him out of countenance, ..."*, which would suggest that we were dealing with a fairly wild-spirited bunch of medical students. However, it is much more likely that the term *pathetic* was used in the older definition of the word, meaning *moving*, which makes more sense.

The portrait is by Andrew Geddes, ARA, a portrait painter who was born in Edinburgh and studied at the Royal Academy. He travelled extensively in Europe, but settled in Edinburgh where he was a member of the *Edinburgh Dilettantes' Club* which met every fortnight in a High Street tavern and included famous painters, such as Sir Henry Raeburn, Sir David Wilkie and Alexander Nasmyth, and literary figures, such as Sir Walter Scott, John Lockhart and James Hogg, the Ettrick Shepherd.

Jamie McGrigor MSP

Sir James McGrigor's direct descendant, visiting the Med-Chi Hall

McGrigor's Obelisk

*erected in 1860 in front of
Marischal College
(before the building of the
Gothic front)*

McGrigor's Obelisk

relocated in 1906 to Duthie Park, Aberdeen

John Grant, Surgeon (1771-1860)

John Grant was the first librarian of the Society. He was appointed on the 7th January 1791, on which day the library was actually begun by Mr Grant presenting the Society with Sydenham's *Opera*. The library went on to become one of the great medical collections. After a long career as military surgeon, Dr Grant retired to Forres where he gave his services to the local people free of charge. He lived to a great age and, as one of the founding members of the Society, was regularly visited by deputations from Aberdeen.

His army career was undistinguished. He was surgeon to the Strathspey Fencibles, and it appears that he never left his native locality.

The portrait was presented to the Society by Dr Grant. The artist is unknown.

John Grant (1771-1860)

Robert Harvey, MD (1770-1825)

(President of the Medico-Chirurgical Society, 1818)

Originally called Robert Donald, he changed his name to Harvey at the behest of his uncle who left him a large sum of money. He was a founder member of the Society and, after graduation, had a successful practice as a physician in Aberdeen. He was made an Honorary Member of the Society in 1805 and, in the same year, he married Mary Gordon. She was the daughter of Alexander Gordon, author of *Treatise on the Epidemic Puerperal Fever of Aberdeen* – the first description of the contagious nature of puerperal fever, nearly 50 years before Semmelweiss.

One of his sons was Alexander Harvey, Professor of Materia Medica at Aberdeen University from 1860 to 1878.

The portrait was presented to the Society by another of his sons, Albert Harvey, MD. In it, he appears as a young man in a sky blue velvet coat, which was affected as a sign of gentility, chiefly in France. The artist is unknown.

Plaque in Belmont Street, Aberdeen
where Alexander Gordon lived

A

TREATISE

ON THE

EPIDEMIC PUERPERAL FEVER

OF

ABERDEEN.

BY

ALEXANDER GORDON, M. D.

PHYSICIAN TO THE DISPENSARY.

LONDON:
PRINTED FOR G. G. AND J. ROBINSON,
PATERNOSTER ROW.
1795.

Alexander Gordon's
*Treatise on the
Epidemic Puerperal
Fever of Aberdeen*

Robert Harvey (1770-1825)

George Kerr (1771-1826)

(President of the Society, 1790)

George Kerr was one of the founders of the Society. After graduation he practised as a physician in Aberdeen. He was Secretary and Treasurer of the Society during its early days, and he and McGrigor were the first Presidents. He was described by a contemporary as of *"sharp, incisive and vigorous mental parts"*. In the way of educated people of his day, he wished to advance knowledge by "disputation", that is to say, by intelligent argument and debate. In 1816, he published a book entitled, *Observations on the Harveian Doctrine of the Circulation of the Blood*, in which he attempted to prove that, although Harvey's conclusions were correct, he had reached them by the wrong methods.

He was one of the five founders who attended the 1794 meeting in London when they wrote to the Society advising them that they should pursue the practice of dissection of the human body and that they should obtain bodies, as was done elsewhere, by the practice of "resurrectionism". The students of the Society followed this advice, which led to the establishment of watch towers and mortsafes throughout the graveyards of the North-East. The practice was officially frowned upon, but unofficially it was permitted. In the minutes there are several mentions of bodies having been obtained and dissections having taken place. The practice of body-snatching was carried out by the students themselves; occasionally, the wealthier students would buy specimens from their less well-off colleagues, but otherwise there was no financial involvement.

The portrait is a copy and was purchased by subscription.

Mortsafes in
Banchory
and Skene
churchyards

Watchtower in Banchory churchyard

George Kerr (1771-1826)

James Moir (1770-1861)

(President of the Medico-Chirurgical Society, 1825, 1832 & 1838)

James Moir was a Physician in Aberdeen and Senior Physician to the Infirmary (1808-1814). His father was the Reverend Dr Moir, a minister of the Established Church in Peterhead, and James was one of 17 children. He was the author of *Notes on Puerperal Fever* (1822). Known as *"Snuffy" Moir* because of his liking for snuff, he was frequently seen in Union Street, walking with one hand behind his back holding his snuff box. He was a founder of the Society and the last to die in 1861. His funeral procession set off from the Medical Hall, the members walking in front of the cortège.

The portrait is by James Giles RSA (1801-1870), and was purchased by subscription.

James Giles (1801–1870) was born in Aberdeen. He was known for his painting skills by the age of 13 and, two years later, was teaching art. He studied anatomy at Marischal College and was friendly with the students of the Society. He later travelled to London, France, Italy and Switzerland. In 1829, he was elected to membership of the Royal Scottish Academy, the first member to have his address outside Edinburgh. He is renowned for his watercolours of Aberdeenshire castles of which he painted 85 in all. It is said that it was his painting that gave Queen Victoria her first view of the old castle of Balmoral.

James Moir (1770-1861)

The Founders' Plaque

This Plaque entitled *"Aberdeen Medico-Chirurgical Society 1789"* lists the twelve Founders of the Society. It is headed by James McGrigor and James Robertson, the two members who played the major part in the foundation of the Society. They had been to Edinburgh and modelled the Society on the Royal Medical Society of Edinburgh (founded 1737). The twelve Founders were:

> James McGrigor
> James Robertson
> Colin Allan
> Robert Donald (Harvey)
> John Gordon
> John Grant
> George Kerr
> Joseph MacKay
> Alex Mitchell
> James Moir
> William Shepherd
> James Smith

It is interesting that six of the Founders pursued military careers, perhaps influenced, as McGrigor was, when impressionable young students.

Portraits of James McGrigor, Robert Donald (Harvey), John Grant, George Kerr and James Moir are displayed in the Society's Hall, and descriptions of these are found with the reproductions of the portraits.

Initially, each member of the Society took it in turns to be President for a meeting.

Colin Allan attended Marischal College as an arts student 1788-92, but did not graduate. He was awarded an MD in 1799. He served as a Regimental Surgeon and eventually became the Principal Medical Officer in Halifax, Nova Scotia. He came from a prosperous family, which gave its name to Allanvale Cemetery and Allan Street in Aberdeen. He was President of the re-constituted Medico-Chirurgical Society in 1820.

James Robertson was another student of arts who did not graduate. He was McGrigor's closest friend and was with him in Edinburgh and in the Iberian Peninsula. He served in Barbados, and while there was wrongly told that McGrigor had lost his life. Robertson then informed The Medical Society, which, with the family, went into mourning; McGrigor was later found alive on another ship.

James Smith was the son of a medical practitioner at Slains, Aberdeenshire. He graduated AM in 1793.

John Gordon, Glenfiddich, was a student of arts but did not graduate. He became a surgeon in the Indian Colonial Service.

Joseph MacKay of Peterculter graduated AM at Marischal College in 1792.

Alexander Mitchell of Glen Isla graduated AM at Marischal College in 1791.

William Shepherd of Virginia graduated AM from Marischal College in 1790, and MD in 1792. He was the first Treasurer of the Society.

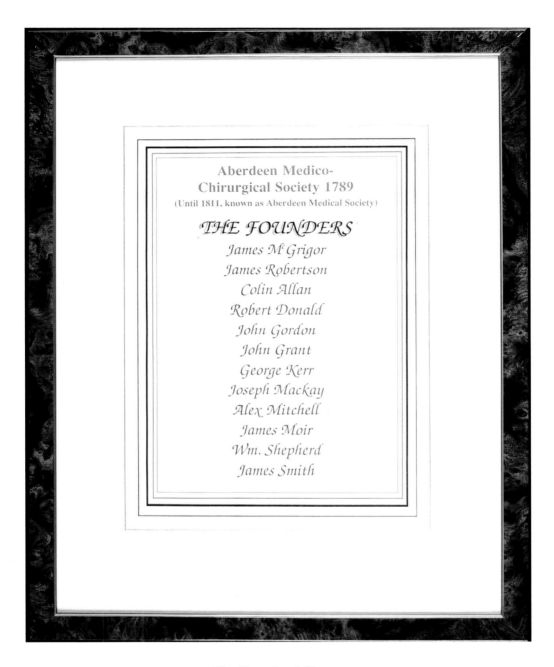

The Founders' Plaque

William Harvey (1578-1657)

"The famous discoverer of the true theory of the circulation of the blood, made known to the world in 1628."

In 1641, Harvey visited Aberdeen, having been sent by King Charles whom he had accompanied to Edinburgh. He was feted by the City Council and awarded the Freedom of the City.

Harvey's predecessor as Chief Royal Physician was Dr Bedwin or Beaton, a Scot who was related to the famous physicians of the Lords of the Isles. Harvey travelled with him to Edinburgh in 1633, thus experiencing an interesting contact with Celtic medicine which at that time was much more advanced than in the Scottish Lowlands and England.

The portrait was presented to the Society by Sir Walter Farquhar, MD of King's College and the son of a Peterhead minister. He was an eminent London physician who attended George III during the King's mental illness.

In a letter dated July 4th, 1815, Sir Walter wrote to the Society – *"Some time ago, Lord Bessborough made me a present of a genuine and undoubted portrait of the great Harvey, and I cannot better dispose of it than by presenting it to your Society, to be placed in your great room as a stimulus to the exertions of your young students in their professional pursuits. I have often and often wished that he had been a Scotchman."*

The painter of the portrait is unknown. It has been copied several times and was photographed at the request of Sir William Osler. The source of the painting has been the subject of much speculation; Dr John Webster, former President of the Society (2004-05), believes it is a copy of the portrait in the Hunterian Collection, University of Glasgow, which is thought to have been painted from life.

William Harvey (1578-1657)

Photograph of the plaque commemorating the event on
30 August 1641 when William Harvey visited
Aberdeen and was made a Free Burgess of Guild

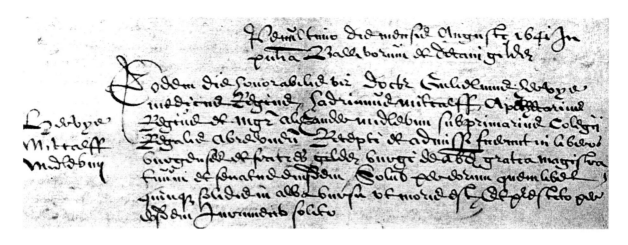

Extract from the minutes of the Town Council of Aberdeen (1641)

Penultimo die mensis Augusti 1641 in
Presentia Ballovorum et decani gilde

Hervye
Mitcalff
Midletun

Eodem die honorabilis vir doctus Gulielmus Herveye,
medicus Regius, hadrianus mitcalff Apothecarius
Regius et magister Alexander midletun subprimarius Colegii
Regalis Abredonensis recepti et admissi fuerunt in liberos
burgenses et frates gilde burgi de aberdonia gratia magistra-
tuum et senatus eiusdem Solutis per eorum quemlibet
quinque solidis in alba bursa ut moris est, Ex prestito ab
eisdem Iuramento solito.

Translation of the entry:

On 30 August 1641 in presence of the Baillies and the dean of guild

Hervye
Mitcalff
Midletun

On the same day the honourable gentleman, the learned William Hervye, Physician to the King, Adrian Mitcalff, Apothecary to the King, and Mr Alexander Midletun, subprincipal of King's College, Aberdeen, were received and admitted as free burgesses and brethren of guild of the Burgh of Aberdeen by grace of the Magistrates and Council of the same, each of them having paid five shillings in a white purse, as is the custom, and having taken the customary oath.

William Livingston, MD (1760-1822)

(Honorary President of the Society, 1791-1812; President of Medico-Chirurgical Society, 1812)

William Livingston was Professor of Medicine at Marischal College 1793-1822.

When the Society was founded, he was senior physician at Aberdeen Royal Infirmary and taught his students there. He was the first qualified member of the profession to be connected with the Society, having been elected Honorary President in 1791. Throughout his life he was a strong supporter of the Society and, when the Society was re-constituted in 1812, he was the first President. In the early years he gave the Society the use of a house of his own, and there the library was stored, meetings were held and dissections carried out. Unfortunately, a resurrected body was discovered there and, owing to the ensuing public scandal, the Society had to move elsewhere.

Dr Livingston was highly regarded as a physician and surgeon. It is recorded that in these pre-anaesthetic days *"a female patient was dismissed cured from the infirmary after having had a cancerous breast amputated by Dr Livingston. It measured 26" in diameter and weighed nine English pounds"*. William Livingston and his father, Thomas, are said to have been *"the makers of the Aberdeen Infirmary"*. Thomas Livingston was its first surgeon, and was sent away to learn how to cut for stone and to do amputations which, together with surgery for cataract (performed in Aberdeen at that time by George Rose who had been taught the technique in Leiden), comprised the entire repertoire of operations. William Livingston was known as *"a 'great grumbler' who constantly complained about defective apparatus"*.

His lasting fame is due to the fact that he treated the poet Byron's clubfoot, with some success, by bandaging the foot in a corrected position. The bandaging caused some discomfort and, to distract him at night, his nurse read to him stories from the Bible. This gave rise later to the *Hebrew Melodies*. Later, Byron moved to England where it is reported that he was treated by a *"mere empirical pretender"*, who turned his foot round by force and screwed it up in a wooden machine, causing him exquisite torture and doing him no good.

Lord Byron

Livingston died in 1822, leaving a legacy and some valuable books to the Society. In the Minutes, it is recorded that *"it was resolved unanimously that the late Dr Livingston, having been the only patron and for a long time the President of the Society, and having contributed in every way to its support and final establishment, Mrs Livingston be requested to permit a copy of his portrait in her possession to be taken for the purpose of the main place in the Hall of the Society"*. The request was granted, and a copy of the original portrait is that now in the possession of the Society. The original portrait, the work of John Moir, was painted in 1826.

John Moir (1741-1818) was the son of a Peterhead Minister. He studied painting in Rome and became renowned as a landscape painter. In later life, he took up portrait painting, among his subjects being the fourth Duke of Gordon, John Stuart and Dr George French.

William Livingston (1760-1822)

George French, MD (1765-1853)

George French was Professor of Chemistry at Marischal College, 1793-1833. He was the nephew of Sir William Fordyce, a successful London physician. After a short career in the army, George French joined his uncle in London, but was apparently unsuccessful there. He returned to Aberdeen where he was one of the two physicians at the Royal Infirmary, and, with William Livingston, he attempted to establish a course of lectures in medicine and surgery in 1786. Due to lack of support, this was abandoned two years later. Dr French was said to have been of a cantankerous nature - *"... a peppery and irascible gentleman, inclined to grouse, and fight with all and sundry"* - and when invited to become an honorary member, he declared publicly that he had no intention of having anything to do with the Society. It appears that he was in dispute with the Society over some unknown matter. Later he became reconciled and, when he died, he left a number of books to the Society's library.

He was not highly regarded as Professor of Chemistry, a subject which had, to the public of those days, *"a suspicion of diablerie"*, as Riddell puts it. In his later years, he gave up teaching, engaging an assistant to take his place whilst still drawing his salary as Professor. He owned a shop in the Upper Kirkgate, selling patent medicines and perfumery, and supplying the Infirmary with medicines and wines, reputedly at inflated prices.

This portrait is also by John Moir, and was also painted in 1826.

George French (1765-1853)

John Stuart (1751-1827)

(Honorary Member of the Society)

Professor John Stuart was Professor of Greek at Marischal College from 1782 until his death. He was a supporter of the Society in its early days, allowing it to meet in his classroom for the first 18 months of the Society's existence. He was admitted as an Honorary Member in 1791. He had a particular interest in Scottish antiquities.

Stuart is described as a frank, kindly man who proved a generous friend to homeless students.

Although he had a large family, his home was always open to members of his class. Because of his lameness, he was affectionately nicknamed *"Dot-and-carry-one"* by his students.

The portrait is by John Moir and was purchased by subscription. The subject's name is misspelt as "Stewart" in the accompanying legend.

John Stuart (1751-1827)

Robert Jamieson, MA, MD (1818-1895)

(President of the Medico-Chirurgical Society, 1856-57)

Robert Jamieson was physician to the Royal Lunatic Asylum (now The Royal Cornhill Hospital) in Aberdeen and later its Superintendent. During his tenure of office, he introduced far-reaching reforms, greatly improving the facilities and the welfare of the patients.

He supervised a new building at the hospital, for a long period thereafter considered to be the last word in mental hospital architecture. He believed that any punishment involving cruelty or injuries to patients was indefensible and campaigned against the use of the cold shower and the rotary chair, which were common practices at that time, instead recommending exercise in the open air, warm baths and occupational therapy. He found "scotch ale" a good hypnotic.

Jamieson was one of the first in this country to give a regular course of lectures on mental diseases recognised by a University. He stated that *"there should be a chair established in every university for the discussion of the subject of the disordered mind; it should embrace the whole subject of mental philosophy, of psychopathology and of moral therapeutics and mental hygiene, with a bearing upon education, upon the development of virtue and the prevention of crime"*.

The portrait is by Sir George Reid, who was the President of the Royal Scottish Academy 1891-1902. In 1891, he was knighted by Queen Victoria at Windsor Castle.

Robert Jamieson (1818-1895)

William Dyce, MD (1770-1835)

(President of the Medico-Chirurgical Society, 1819 & 1829)

After graduation, William Dyce was appointed as physician to the dispensary, succeeding that outstanding doctor, Alexander Gordon. He probably owned the first doctor's carriage in Aberdeen, supposedly a gift from one of his sons, which was irreverently christened *"the pill box"*. He inherited the property of Cuttlehill near Aberdeen. From 1811 to 1826 he was Lecturer in midwifery at Marischal College. Dyce was described as a tall, spare, stately man, *"reticent and unbending"*. He was made an Honorary Member of the Society in 1799 and was President in 1819 and 1829.

He continued the practice of the teaching of midwifery, which had been begun by Dr Skene in the mid-eighteenth century. It was during his time (1827), nearly one hundred years before official certification of midwives, that the Society established a register of midwives and issued certificates after examination. No member of the Society would recognise a midwife unless she was registered. The subjects of the examination were: *(i) Anatomy and dimensions of the pelvis and child, and its foetal appendages and circulation, (ii) Diseases incidental to pregnancy, (iii) Management of labour, (iv) After treatment and diseases consequent, (v) Management of children and their common complaints, (vi) Bleeding and management of leeches, (vii) Use of a catheter.*

The portrait is by his son, William Dyce, a painter of considerable renown who is regarded as a pioneer of state art education. He graduated MA from Marischal College at the age of 16, and started to study medicine, then theology, as his father did not encourage his real interest which was in painting. However, his father relented, and young William was allowed to study at the Royal Scottish Academy and then London and abroad. He returned to Edinburgh to take up portrait painting, since he could not get enough patrons to support his speciality of religious paintings. He again moved to London where he was elected to The Royal Academy and was appointed the first Professor of the Theory of Fine Arts at King's College, London. He advised on the formation of the National Gallery. At the invitation of the Prince Consort, he undertook the painting of frescos in the House of Lords and in the Queen's Robing Room in the Palace of Westminster. He has been described as intolerant and forthright in his views, and some critics felt that he did not achieve his full potential because he dispersed his talents too widely.

The portrait was given to the Society by another of William Dyce's sons (there were 11 children), Robert Dyce, who was the Professor of Midwifery after the union of King's and Marischal in 1860. Thus he continued the prominence of the Dyce family that can be traced back to charters granted to John de Diss in 1457, whose estates probably gave their name to the village (now suburb) of Dyce outside Aberdeen.

William Dyce (1770-1835)

George Watt (1762 -?)

George Watt attended the arts class at Marischal College, but did not graduate, which was not an uncommon practice in the eighteenth century. Nevertheless, he built up a reputation as a skilful and daring surgeon and attracted apprentices from far and wide. He is described as industrious, greedy and a wit. He practised in Aberdeenshire, and there was an ongoing rivalry between him and the Aberdeen surgeons. A story is told that, having met a country man near Dudwick one day, he performed upon him, then and there, a successful operation for removal of a tumour on the head, which the Aberdeen Infirmary surgeon had declined to do; *"There"*, said Dr Watt to the grateful patient, *"I've done what the Aberdeen doctors can't do. Just you go and tell folk that if they ask who cured you, you can say it was Geordie Watt"*.

His only child, George, a Writer to the Signet, died of cholera contracted when attending the funeral of a friend who had died of the disease. In his memory, Dr Watt gifted money to establish a house of refuge. Over the years, a surplus of the gift was used to buy the site at Old Mill, where a Poor House was erected, and eventually, in 1927, Woodend Hospital.

The portrait, by James Giles, was presented to the Society by his grandnephew, Mr Andrew Anderson. He is depicted as an old gentleman in a swallow-tail coat, seated in a chair, with a plan of his lands in his right hand and a statue behind him representing charity.

George Watt (1762 -?)

David Hutcheon (1765-1832)

(Honorary Member and Treasurer of the Medico-Chirurgical Society)

David Hutcheon was born in Fetteresso, where his father was the minister. He was lamed for life when a schoolhouse roof collapsed upon him during a storm. He became an Advocate in Aberdeen, and is said to have been one of the last men in Aberdeen to wear the old dress of knee breeches and silk stockings. Elected an Honorary Member of the Medico-Chirurgical Society in 1813, he acted for many years as its Treasurer and Law Agent, free of charge.

The portrait is by James Giles RSA, and was presented to the Society by David Hutcheon himself.

A second portrait by William Dyce RA (1830) is also in the Society's Hall, commissioned by the Society. It had been put in storage after Giles' portrait was put up, and was found by Thomas Morrice, the Hall keeper, "covered with dust and dirt" in a cupboard.

David Hutcheon (1765-1832)
by William Dyce

David Hutcheon (1765-1832)
by James Giles

Joseph Williamson, MD (? -1860)

(President of the Medico-Chirurgical Society, 1848)

Joseph Williamson was a physician in Aberdeen. He was Secretary of the Society from 1837 to 1841 and, in 1848, was elected President.

His careful handwritten entries on the Society's meetings are still clearly legible today. He suffered from ill health during the whole of his working life. It is said that on the day before he died, he visited a poor woman, with a baby, who offered him a sovereign as all she could give for his professional attendance on her. He refused the fee which, in a spirit of independent pride, was re-offered; the doctor bent over the child's cradle and put the money under the pillow, to be found after he left.

After he died in 1860, a special meeting of the Society was held so that members could have an opportunity of showing their respect for the memory of Dr Joseph Williamson by attending his funeral. It is recorded that later *"the members joined the funeral procession of Dr Joseph Williamson opposite the Society Hall and preceded the body to the grave"*.

The portrait was presented to the Society by his sister, Miss Eliza Williamson. It was painted by James Giles, RSA.

Extract from the Minute Book of the Society in Joseph Williamson's handwriting (1840)

Joseph Williamson (? -1860)

John C Ogilvie, MD (1784-1839)

(President of the Medico-Chirurgical Society, 1813, 1827 & 1831)

John Charles Ogilvie was present at the first meeting of the reconstructed Society in 1812 and, in 1813, he became its second President in succession to Professor William Livingston. He was also President in 1827 and 1831. For many years, he acted as Secretary and produced a complete catalogue of the Library.

He was always immaculately dressed in a long coat, frilled shirt, knee breeches, black silk hose and silver buckled shoes, with his hair powdered and tied with a ribbon. His son, Dr George Ogilvie-Forbes, was the first Professor of Physiology in the University of Aberdeen after the union of King's and Marischal in 1860.

The portrait is by James Giles and was purchased by subscription.

John Ogilvie (1784-1839)

Rev. **William Laing**, MA, MD (? -1812)

(Honorary Member of the Medico-Chirurgical Society)

William Laing was a Minister in Peterhead, and the author of *An Account of Peterhead, its Mineral Well, Air and Neighbourhood.* As well as serving the community as Minister, he acted as its physician.

Elected an Honorary Member of the Society, he contributed one guinea to buy a book for the library *"as a small memorandum of indelible affection"*. He was described as a sociable, friendly man of broad, liberal views, and he was interested in chemistry. It seems strange today, but, in his time, Peterhead was a popular spa town, frequented by the landed gentry who came to take the waters and to consult Dr Laing, who was regarded as an excellent doctor.

The portrait is by James Giles.

Rev. William Laing (? -1812)

Sir John Struthers, MD, FRCS, LLD, PRCSEd (1823-1899)

(President of the Medico-Chirurgical Society, 1884-85)

Sir John Struthers, an Edinburgh graduate, was Professor of Anatomy at Aberdeen from 1863 to 1889, during which time he made a huge contribution to the advancement of medicine and medical education. He was also a surgeon, but gave up clinical practice upon moving to Aberdeen. When he was appointed, he was appalled by the limited facilities available for the teaching of anatomy and set about improving them. When he retired in 1889, his Department was said to be of unequalled excellence in Britain. He was the first Chairman of the Education Committee of the General Medical Council and was largely responsible for the introduction of the modern five-year medical curriculum. A follower of Darwin, he carried out extensive research in comparative anatomy, collecting a large museum of specimens illustrating the theory of evolution, and included these theories in his teaching of Anatomy – to the benefit and stimulus of students such as Arthur Keith, the famous anatomist, who attributed the success of his career to Struthers' Darwinian teachings. However, some of his classmates (as J Scott Riddell recalls, referring to himself and the Professor of Midwifery) *"could not imbibe the Darwinian milk (Struthers' Brand), with avidity, being strict Presbyterians, both fresh from exhaustive and exhausting courses of Moral Philosophy, and Christian Evidences; both also fond of field sports, for which the distinguished Anatomist had no use whatsoever; and both inclined, on occasion, to rapid* en bloc *dissection, rather than the meticulous use of the scalpel, in what appeared to be unimportant areas."*

Struthers' interest in comparative anatomy involved him in a number of well-publicised incidents. When a whale was washed up on the beaches around Aberdeen, Struthers would have the carcass removed to Marischal College for dissection and display to the students. The smell from these activities was legendary. The skeleton of a Sei whale hung in the entrance of the "Drain" (the Anatomy Department in Marischal College) until 1967, when it was moved to the Zoology Department where it is still said to drip oil if the weather is very warm. He was also involved in the famous Tay whale incident, which was subsequently immortalised by William McGonagall in his individual style of poetry.

He joined the Society in 1864 and cast covetous eyes on a skeleton of a crocodile in the Society's museum. This had been gifted to the Society in 1822, as *"an aligator* (sic)*"*, by Dr Alexander, of Prince of Wales Island in Malaya, who (as Riddell puts it) *"must have had rather an exciting Country practice"*. He asked permission to have it removed to his Department to have it cleaned, but failed to return the skeleton to the Society. There followed a long-running battle over many years between members of the Society and Professor Struthers regarding the ownership of the skeleton. Eventually, Professor Struthers was forced to return the specimen by Court Order. He resigned from the Society but rejoined six years later. In 1884 he was President of the Society and again tried to obtain possession of the crocodile, but again he failed. It was not until 1956 that the skeleton was presented to the Anatomy Department of the University.

Struthers further risked the wrath of the Society in 1886 when he became the first President to break the tradition of delivering the annual Presidential address *"owing to pressure of work"* – the classic Professorial excuse.

The portrait from which the engraving is taken was painted by Sir George Reid.

Engraving of Professor Sir John Struthers (1823-1899)

Sir John Struthers.
(*by Sir George Reid RSA,*
by permission, University
of Aberdeen)

Cartoon of Professor Struthers
as the Rag-and-Bone Man
From Bon Accord II, 13 November 1886

Struthers was the object of some derision
for his support of Darwinism, and his
comparative anatomy collections.

Photograph of the crocodile
(by permission of the *Press & Journal*)

Sir Alexander Ogston, KCVO, MB, MD, LLD Glasgow & Aberdeen (1846-1929)

Regius Professor of Surgery (1882-1909)

(President of the Medico-Chirurgical Society, 1905)

Alexander Ogston was a member of a distinguished Aberdeen family. He graduated MB in 1865 and MD the following year, both with highest honours. A polymath and polyglot, his knowledge of languages enabled him to attend the foremost medical centres in Europe and to meet the leaders of medical research of his day. He was one of the first to appreciate the importance of Lister's theory of antisepsis, and his adoption of this technique enabled him to be a pioneer of orthopaedic and abdominal surgery. His enquiring mind led him to investigate the cause of sepsis, and in a series of careful experiments he demonstrated the part played by micro-organisms in wound infection and blood poisoning. He named the organism, which appeared as grape-like clusters, *'staphylococcus'*, and distinguished it from the *streptococcus*, which appeared in chains. On the continent, this work was acclaimed but in Britain it was received coldly, and as a result he had to give his first paper in Germany, where his work was enthusiastically received. The editor of the British Medical Journal asked, *"Can any good thing come out of Aberdeen?"*[1], and the Journal refused to publish some of Ogston's later papers. In Britain, his name stands supreme as the only research worker who produced contributions which led to the understanding of pathogenic bacteria in the early days of bacteriology.

When he applied for the Regius Chair of Surgery, he had numerous testimonials from all over Britain and Europe, including many of the leading surgeons of his day. However, there are two that stand out and are a mark that any

teacher would be proud and honoured to have: one was signed by over 200 medical graduates of Aberdeen, and the other by 250 medical students, both supporting him most warmly.

Among his many other achievements was the reform of the Army and Navy medical services. He attended as an observer in the Sudan Wars in 1885 and the Boer War, and he campaigned for modernisation of training and equipment of the army medical services. He was called to give evidence before several committees investigating the causes of the disastrous medical conditions which existed at the time of the Boer Wars. His campaign was successful so that the RAMC was able to face the unprecedented demands of the 1914-18 war as a well-trained and equipped body. Ogston himself acted as surgeon in various theatres during the war, finally retiring at the age of 74.

His portrait is by George Fiddes Watt. The late Ronnie Cumming wrote a good biographical snapshot of the painter in the *Bicentennial History*:

> George Fiddes Watt was born in Aberdeen in 1873, living his early life in Stanley Street. He left school at the age of fourteen and was turned down for jobs as a message boy because of a speech impediment. Eventually he obtained a post as a litho artist with the *Northern Advertiser*, attending Gray's School of Art in the evenings. He described how he used to rise at 3 a.m. to paint in Rubislaw Den. Later he moved to Edinburgh and studied at the Royal Scottish Academy Life School, winning the Chalmers Bursary and McLean Watters Medal. On one occasion, having run out of money, he came on leave

---

[1] Referring to St John, chapter 1, verse 46 "Can there any good thing come out of Nazareth?" Philip replied, "Come and see." But the distinguished editor did not come to Aberdeen.

Professor Sir Alexander Ogston (1846-1929)

travelling in the cab of a train by permission of the engine-driver who was a friend of his. He was elected an Associate of the Royal Scottish Academy in 1910, achieving full membership in 1924. Many people alive today remember him as a well-known figure in Union Street, tall, with a van Dyck beard, wearing an Inverness cape and carrying a long silver topped cane. He was awarded an Honorary LLD by Aberdeen University in 1955 and died in 1960 at 73 Cranford Road. Among notable personages who sat for him were Lord Asquith, Lord Haldane, Earl Grey, Lord Balfour, of Burleigh and the Archbishop of York.

Following Ogston's death in 1929, the Secretary reported that *"a wreath of bay leaves had been laid below the portrait of Sir Alex. Ogston"*.

A Bajan of Marischal College of 1859-60.

Drawing of a bajan of the University of Aberdeen
(It is commonly assumed that this is a depiction of the young Alexander Ogston as a student.)

Signed photograph of Professor Ogston

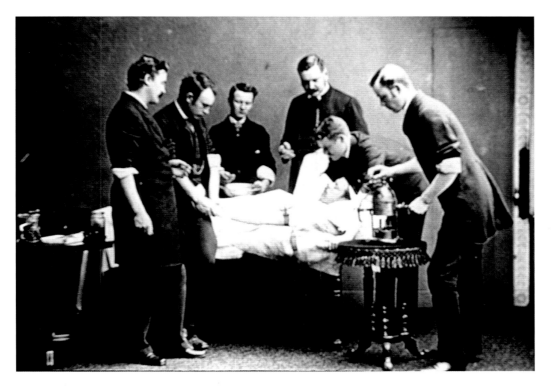

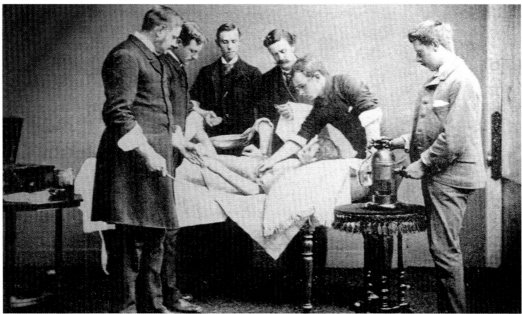

The two posed photographs above show an operation in Aberdeen using Ogston's antiseptic spray, based on Lister's work – Ogston was one of the first surgeons to adopt his principles and practice. Professor Ogston is on the extreme left in the top photograph, and third from the right in the bottom one.

Ogston's spray

Microscope from Professor
Ogston's Department
(lit by internal oil lamp)

Aberdeen Royal
Infirmary at Woolmanhill
(1930)

Ward in Aberdeen Royal
Infirmary at Woolmanhill

Operating Theatre in
Aberdeen Royal
Infirmary at Woolmanhill

Sir Patrick Manson, GCMG, MD, DSc, FRS, LLD (1844-1922)

"The Father of Tropical Medicine"

Born at Oldmeldrum, Patrick Manson graduated from Aberdeen University and went to the East in 1866, where he discovered that the disease of elephantiasis was spread by mosquitoes, the first description of an insect-borne disease. He went on to make many other discoveries in tropical medicine and, in a long correspondence, he guided Sir Ronald Ross in his experiments to show the role of the mosquito as the transmitter of malaria. He had two infected mosquitoes brought to London where they were allowed to bite two healthy Londoners – one of them his own son. After the due period of incubation both of these developed typical malaria. He then organised an expedition to Italy to a particularly malarious area. In a hut protected by mosquito-proof gauze, three persons lived during four months of the malaria season without developing the disease, in striking contrast to the unprotected persons outside.

While in Hong Kong, with two other Aberdeen graduates, he established the Medical School for the Chinese. The two others were Sir James Cantlie and Sir Kai Ho Kai; the latter was a Chinaman from Hong Kong who studied medicine in Aberdeen and graduated there.

After returning to London, Sir Patrick Manson was mainly responsible for the establishment of the London School of Tropical Medicine in 1897 and he was appointed its first head. He was the author of *"Manual of Tropical Diseases"*, the standard work on the subject.

The portrait is by Violet Bowie and is a copy. It was given to the Society by her brother, Dr Harold Bowie.

Portrait of Professor Sir Patrick Manson
(reproduced with permission of the *Library & Archives Service, London School of Hygiene & Tropical Medicine*)

Professor Sir Patrick Manson (1844-1922)

J J R Macleod, MBChB, DPH, DSC, FRCP, FRS, LLD (1876–1935)

John James Rickard Macleod was born in Perthshire, but moved with his family to Aberdeen when he was seven years old. He was educated at Aberdeen Grammar School and Aberdeen University, graduating with honourable distinction in 1898. As a postgraduate student, he studied in Leipzig and Aberdeen. In 1903, at the age of 27, he was appointed Professor of Physiology at Western University, Cleveland.

In 1918, he moved to Toronto as Professor of Physiology and it was in his laboratory there that insulin was discovered. Macleod was jointly awarded the Nobel Prize, but the discovery was followed by years of controversy, and Macleod's reputation suffered as a result. He did not defend himself and eventually, in 1928, he retired from the Chair in Toronto to become Regius Professor of Physiology at Aberdeen. It was not until 1982 when a Canadian historian, Michael Bliss, published his book, *"The Discovery of Insulin"*, that his reputation was restored and he took his rightful place as co-discoverer of insulin with Banting, Best and Collip. The large lecture hall in the new science building in Toronto is named the J J R Macleod Auditorium.

His biography, *"J J R Macleod, The Co-discoverer of Insulin"* by Michael J Williams, physician, Aberdeen Royal Infirmary was published by the Royal College of Physicians of Edinburgh in 1993. A copy is in the Society's library.

As with Manson's portrait, the portrait of Macleod is by Violet Bowie and is a copy. It was given to the Society by her brother, Dr Harold Bowie.

Professor J J R Macleod

Professor Macleod's Nobel Prize for Medicine Medal (1923)

Professor J J R Macleod (1876-1935)

Matthew Hay, MB, CM (Hons), MD, LLD (1855-1932)

Matthew Hay was born in Slamannan, the son of a colliery owner. He had a brilliant career at Dollar Academy and the Universities of Glasgow and Edinburgh, and won innumerable prizes. From 1878 to 1883, he was Assistant Professor in Materia Medica in Edinburgh and studied in Munich and Berlin, quickly making his mark in academic medicine. In 1883, he was appointed to the Chair of Medical Logic and Jurisprudence (Forensic Medicine) in Aberdeen. His application had been supported by 10 Fellows of the Royal Society and 522 students. He was just 27 years of age. He made many contributions to the improvement of public health care in Aberdeen and district and also achieved fame as an expert in Forensic Medicine. It is impossible in a short description to describe his achievements in these fields; however the following story typifies the man.

Professor Matthew Hay

In the true spirit of the Public Health detective, he investigated an epidemic of typhus in Aberdeen in 1905 and demonstrated, for the first time, that the disease was transmitted by body vermin. He then made two "mistakes" – his only written account of his findings was in his local annual report, and he referred to the vermin as *"fleas"*. Four years later, in 1909, the Frenchman, Charles Nicolle, showed that the vermin concerned in the European variety of typhus was the body louse, thereby winning renown and a Nobel Prize. In keeping with Hay's natural modesty and indifference to fame, his only comment was, *"What does it matter who gets the credit so long as lives are saved?"*

Matthew Hay's abiding legacy is due to his vision in proposing the Joint Hospitals Scheme at Foresterhill. As early as 1900, he had identified Foresterhill as the ideal situation for a co-ordinated hospital scheme, including The Childrens' Hospital, the Royal Infirmary, the Maternity Hospital and the Medical School. On the 6th February 1920, with Sir Ashley Mackintosh in the Chair, *"Preliminary arrangements were made for holding a special meeting of the Society to be devoted to a discussion on the question of a hospital accommodation for Aberdeen and District, Dr Matthew Hay to open the discussion, to be followed by Sir Henry Gray and Dr A W Mackintosh"*. This meeting was held on the 20th February and was followed by a second meeting of the Society with other members of the medical profession in the North of Scotland on the 10th March, where it was resolved that *"there is a growing and clamant need in Aberdeen for largely increased hospital accommodation of the most modern type"*.

This was followed by a conference of the Society with the Governors of the Hospital for Sick Children, the Royal Infirmary, The University of Aberdeen and the Town Council (where there was strong support from the Lord Provost, Sir Andrew Lewis) on the 20th April, when the following statement was issued:

Engraving of Professor Matthew Hay (1855-1932)

"The following resolutions, which were proposed by Sir Ashley Mackintosh as President of the Medico-Chirurgical Society and seconded by Mr George Davidson as Director of The Royal Infirmary, were unanimously accepted by the Conference, namely:

1. *That the question of increased and improved hospital accommodation in Aberdeen be taken back for consideration by each of the bodies represented at the Meeting.*

2. *That the heads of each of these bodies, when their deliberations were completed so far as possible send in a post or précis of their conclusions to the President of the Medico-Chirurgical Society, who will then call a meeting of those heads in order to correlate the various reports for submission to an adjourned meeting of the Conference".*

After many vicissitudes, the Joint Hospitals Scheme was completed in 1938 with the opening of the Medical School. The Children's Hospital had been opened in 1929, the Royal Infirmary in 1936 and the Maternity Hospital in 1938. The new Matthew Hay Project, at present in its construction stage, will be a suitable reminder of the vision of Matthew Hay in providing Aberdeen with an unrivalled University and Hospital complex.

After the initial meetings, Matthew Hay took little part in the planning and development of his Joint Hospitals Scheme. He died in 1932 before its completion. His role as the chief medical proponent of the scheme was taken over by Sir Ashley Mackintosh who strove relentlessly to bring about its completion.

Matthew Hay's portrait was executed by Charles Simms RA (1873-1928). The original hangs in the Picture Gallery of Marischal College. A replica presented by his family is in the headquarters building of NHS Grampian.

Portrait of Professor Matthew Hay (1855-1932)
(by permission of *NHS Grampian*)

Aberdeen Infirmary (1742)

Aberdeen Royal Infirmary at Woolmanhill
(1906)

Aberdeen Royal Infirmary at Foresterhill
(artist's impression)

Aberdeen Royal Infirmary at Foresterhill
(under construction)

Sir Ashley W Mackintosh, KCVO, MA, MB ChB, FRCPE, LLD (1868-1937)

Physician to the Royal Household in Scotland, Regius Professor of Medicine (1912-1929)

(President of the Medico-Chirurgical Society, 1919-20)

Ashley Mackintosh was, in all likelihood, Aberdeen's most brilliant medical graduate. He entered the University as first Bursar, graduated MA, MB ChB and MD all with highest honours and won innumerable prizes. He could easily have been a mathematician (a great interest that he shared with his father, the Minister at Deskford); however, he did not produce any great contributions to the medical literature. As Professor of Medicine, his skill and dedication to teaching were unequalled, and no-one before or since has inspired such affection and respect in his students - *"He raised the standard of Aberdeen Medical School to its highest peak"*. This is illustrated by the dinner that was arranged by a London committee of his old students to mark his retirement, which saw 116 attending to express their thanks to their teacher.

He was President of the Medico-Chirurgical Society when Matthew Hay presented his Joint Hospitals Scheme and, from then until its fruition, he was its dedicated promoter, largely responsible for its success. He presented the Society with its gown and golf cup, the latter for annual competition by members of the Society. At the presentation to mark his retirement, Dr Henry Peterkin declared that Sir Ashley was *"one of the most powerful influences for good which we have ever had in the medical world in Aberdeen"*.

When he retired, the Society appointed a committee to raise funds for a portrait. Two portraits were painted by John B Souter, brother of Dr W Clark Souter (President of the Medico-Chirurgical Society, 1932); one was presented to Sir Ashley, and one to the University. Excess money raised was donated by Sir Ashley for the benefit of students. After his death his portrait was given to the Society by his sister, Miss Edith Mackintosh.

John Bulloch Souter was an Aberdonian who earned his living as a portrait painter in London. Among his subjects were many famous stage personalities, including Ivor Novello, Gladys Cooper and Fay Compton.

Professor Sir Ashley W Mackintosh (1868-1937)

Sir John Marnoch, KCVO, MA, MB, LLD (1867-1936)

Surgeon to the Royal Household in Scotland, Regius Professor of Surgery (1909-1932)

(President of the Medico-Chirurgical Society, 1909-10)

Sir John Marnoch was born in Aberdeen and attended Aberdeen Grammar School. He graduated MA and MB CM with the highest honours in 1891; he was one of the last to qualify under the CM degree, which about this time became ChB. His early career was in general practice, but he also carried out research under Professor MacWilliam in the Department of Physiology, and under Professor Hamilton in the Department of Pathology. He went on to become Consultant Surgeon and, from 1909 to 1932, was Professor of Surgery.

As a teacher he gained a wide reputation and he contributed many papers to medical journals. He was renowned as a skilful surgeon, being one of the first surgeons to operate freely in the abdominal cavity, and he was reputed to perform a straightforward appendicectomy in six minutes. Many honours were conferred on him. He was appointed Honorary Surgeon to His Majesty's household in Scotland, became a CVO in 1915 and a KCVO in 1928. He was awarded an LLD by Aberdeen University in 1932. He was also known as an accomplished cellist.

In 1914, in a nursing home in Aberdeen, he carried out an appendicectomy on Prince Albert, later George VI. The Prince made an uneventful recovery. A number of letters, telegrams and reports, including several from his father George V, were passed on to the Society by Sir John's daughter and are now amongst the Society's collection. They are described later.

When he died in 1936, the President of the Society, Dr J Johnston, described Sir John as *"a perfect gentleman, gracious and gentle by nature, and of refined tastes; in all his dealings honourable and upright, helpful to his friends, generous to the poor, considerate and charitable in his judgement of others."*

A Council Meeting dated 1 March 1956 records the acquisition of Sir John's portrait by the Society: *"Dr Richards, as one of the Trustees of the Estate of Sir John Marnoch, intimated that his daughter had offered to the Society his portrait in oils. The Council gratefully accepted the portrait. The Secretary would acknowledge the gift".*

The artist is unknown.

Professor Sir John Marnoch (1867-1936)

David W Finlay, BA, MD, LLD Aberdeen & Yale University (1840-1923)

(President of the Medico-Chirurgical Society, 1901-02)

David White Finlay was Professor of Medicine at Aberdeen from 1891 to 1912. A respected physician and teacher, he did not undertake any medical research, but he was greatly interested in improving the conditions of the poor by social reform.

He was born near Glasgow and had a lifetime interest in yacht racing, about which he wrote a book, a copy of which is in the Society's library.

The portrait is signed R C C 1906. The artist has not been identified definitively, but Professor Lewis D Ritchie (President of the Society, 2003-04) thinks that it may well be Robert Cree Crawford (1842-1924) - almost an exact contemporary of Finlay. He had a reputation for his portraits, including those of leading academics, and exhibited regularly at both the Royal Academy and the Royal Scottish Academy.

.

Professor David Finlay (1840-1923)

The Medico-Chirurgical Society members in 1908

This group photographic montage contains many of the famous names that appear elsewhere in this book, including Mackintosh, Hay, Ogston, Marnoch, Lister, Scott Riddell, Stephenson, Finlay, Cash, MacWilliam, Rorie, *etc.* This period perhaps reflects one of the golden ages of Aberdeen medicine.

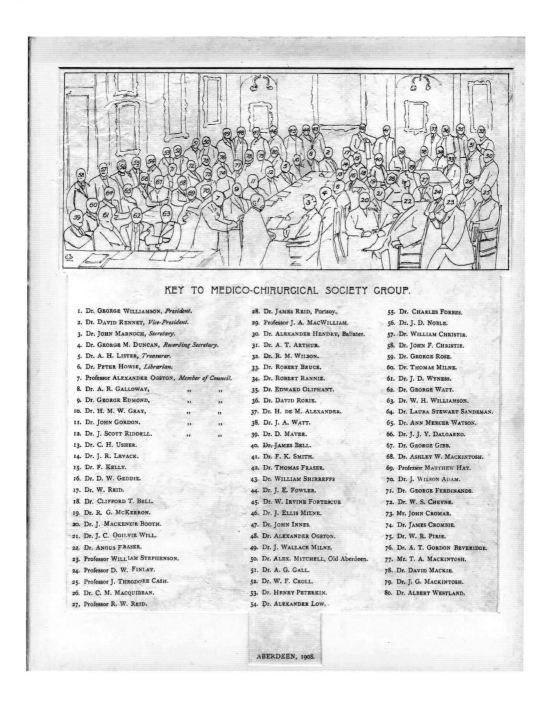

KEY TO MEDICO-CHIRURGICAL SOCIETY GROUP.

1. Dr. George Williamson, *President.*
2. Dr. David Rennet, *Vice-President.*
3. Dr. John Marnoch, *Secretary.*
4. Dr. George M. Duncan, *Recording Secretary.*
5. Dr. A. H. Lister, *Treasurer.*
6. Dr. Peter Howie, *Librarian.*
7. Professor Alexander Ogston, *Member of Council.*
8. Dr. A. R. Galloway,   „   „
9. Dr. George Edmond,   „   „
10. Dr. H. M. W. Gray,   „   „
11. Dr. John Gordon.   „   „
12. Dr. J. Scott Riddell,   „   „
13. Dr. C. H. Usher.
14. Dr. J. R. Levack.
15. Dr. F. Kelly.
16. Dr. D. W. Geddie.
17. Dr. W. Reid.
18. Dr. Clifford T. Bell.
19. Dr. R. G. McKerron.
20. Dr. J. Mackenzie Booth.
21. Dr. J. C. Ogilvie Will.
22. Dr. Angus Fraser.
23. Professor William Stephenson.
24. Professor D. W. Finlay.
25. Professor J. Theodore Cash.
26. Dr. C. M. Macquibean.
27. Professor R. W. Reid.
28. Dr. James Reid, Portsoy.
29. Professor J. A. MacWilliam.
30. Dr. Alexander Hendry, Ballater.
31. Dr. A. T. Arthur.
32. Dr. R. M. Wilson.
33. Dr. Robert Bruce.
34. Dr. Robert Rannie.
35. Dr. Edward Oliphant.
36. Dr. David Rorie.
37. Dr. H. de M. Alexander.
38. Dr. J. A. Watt.
39. Dr. D. Maver.
40. Dr. James Bell.
41. Dr. F. K. Smith.
42. Dr. Thomas Fraser.
43. Dr. William Shirreffs
44. Dr. J. E. Fowler.
45. Dr. W. Irvine Fortescue
46. Dr. J. Ellis Milne.
47. Dr. John Innes.
48. Dr. Alexander Ogston.
49. Dr. J. Wallace Milne.
50. Dr. Alex. Mitchell, Old Aberdeen.
51. Dr. A. G. Gall.
52. Dr. W. F. Croll.
53. Dr. Henry Peterkin.
54. Dr. Alexander Low.
55. Dr. Charles Forbes.
56. Dr. J. D. Noble.
57. Dr. William Christie.
58. Dr. John F. Christie.
59. Dr. George Rose.
60. Dr. Thomas Milne.
61. Dr. J. D. Wyness.
62. Dr. George Watt.
63. Dr. W. H. Williamson.
64. Dr. Laura Stewart Sandeman.
65. Dr. Ann Mercer Watson.
66. Dr. J. J. V. Dalgarno.
67. Dr. George Gibb.
68. Dr. Ashley W. Mackintosh.
69. Professor Matthew Hay.
70. Dr. J. Wilson Adam.
71. Dr. George Ferdinands.
72. Dr. W. S. Cheyne.
73. Mr. John Cromar.
74. Dr. James Crombie.
75. Dr. W. R. Pirie.
76. Dr. A. T. Gordon Beveridge.
77. Mr. T. A. Mackintosh.
78. Dr. David Mackie.
79. Dr. J. G. Mackintosh.
80. Dr. Albert Westland.

ABERDEEN, 1908.

J Patrick S Nicoll, MB, MD (1866-1926)

Dr John Patrick Smith Nicoll was the son of a congregational Minister in Rhynie. After graduating MB and MD at Aberdeen, he spent practically the whole of his adult life in the East End of London in devoted and selfless work on behalf of the women and children of the district. At the time of his death he was Senior Physician at Queen Mary's Hospital, and it was largely owing to his efforts that this great modern hospital evolved out of the small dispensary which had previously served the district. In 1927, the Nicoll Memorial at the hospital was opened by Her Majesty the Queen.

Every summer he returned to Rhynie and accompanied the local doctor on his rounds, looking after his gig and horses while the doctor attended to his patients. He left a legacy to found the hospital at Rhynie, which gave yeoman service to the district until it was closed in 1957.

The portrait is by John B Souter and was gifted to the Society by Miss K M N Smith of Aberdeen.

Patrick Nicoll (1866-1926)

Sir Alexander Greig Anderson, KCVO, MA, MD, LLD (1885-1961)

Honorary Physician to the King's Household in Scotland

(President of the Medico-Chirurgical Society, 1947-48)

A G Anderson graduated in 1909 with highest honours. After service in the First World War, he was appointed Physician to the Royal Infirmary and, from 1936 to 1955, he was Honorary Physician to the King's Household in Scotland. After he retired in 1945 he devoted his energy to the welfare of the old and acted as physician to Morningfield Hospital. He was the first geriatric physician in Aberdeen. An imposing figure, he had an immense influence on medicine during his tenure in office.

The following incident illustrates Sir Alexander's powerful personality. The date is 1946. His habit was to be met by his house physician when he drove up to the Infirmary entrance in the morning. His houseman opened the door of his car to let him out, took his briefcase and walked with him up to the ward. On this occasion, Sir Alexander was followed into the car park by a policeman who approached him and said, *"Excuse me Sir, but are you aware that you were driving down Ashgrove Road at 52 miles an hour? I shall have to charge you, etc."* Sir Alexander drew himself up to his full height, looked down his hooked nose and said *"BOY, GO AWAY"* and the young policeman turned, entered his car and drove off.

The signed etching is by Malcolm Osborne, RA, Professor of Engraving at the Royal College of Art. His etchings are much sought after by collectors. This etching was gifted to the Society in 1950.

ALEXANDER GREIG ANDERSON
PHYSICIAN IN ABERDEEN

Etching of Sir Alexander Greig Anderson (1885-1961)

Sir Dugald Baird, MD, FRCOG, DPH (1899-1986)

(President of the Medico-Chirurgical Society, 1964-65)

Dugald Baird was the outstanding obstetrician of his day. Appalled by the conditions of mothers and children in the Glasgow slums, he spent his life campaigning for improvement. As Professor of Midwifery in Aberdeen from 1937 to 1965, he carried out many reforms. By the use of statistics and the help of scientists from other disciplines, he transformed the maternity services and set a pattern followed throughout the country. He campaigned relentlessly for the *"5th Freedom"* – the freedom from the tyranny of excessive fertility. He also established the first screening service for cervical cancer for a population in Britain, providing a model for other areas.

He received a string of honorary degrees from other Universities and many honours. The excellence of his Department was recognised by the fact that at least twenty-six members of his staff became professors throughout Britain and abroad.

Both Sir Dugald and his wife, Lady May Baird, were honoured with the Freedom of the City of Aberdeen in 1966.

The portrait is by Alberto Morrocco, who studied in Aberdeen and became Head of Painting at Duncan of Jordanstone College of Art, Dundee. He was elected a member of the Royal Scottish Academy in 1962. His paintings are found in many galleries, both in this country and abroad.

Professor Dugald Baird

Professor Sir Dugald Baird (1899-1986)

Robert D Lockhart, MB, MD, LLD, FSA (Scotland), FRSE (1894-1987)

(President of the Medico-Chirurgical Society, 1951-52)

Robert Douglas Lockhart was Professor of Anatomy at Aberdeen from 1938 to 1964. Under his guidance, anatomy teaching reached a perfection not attained before or since. He transformed the department, greatly improving facilities for teaching and dissection. His specimens were skilfully prepared, and illustrated by the artist Alberto Morrocco. Everything had to be of the highest standard. With his assistants, Doctors Hamilton and Fyfe, he produced a classic textbook, *The Anatomy of the Human Body*. This book was a worldwide success. It was translated into Spanish, Italian and Portuguese and it was made a standard text in hospital libraries in the USA.

His teaching emphasised the living and the practical; *"to teach you have first to entertain"* was a favourite saying and was a policy followed in his carefully prepared lectures. Question and answer sessions were enlivened by "catch-phrases", such as *"Steady the Buffs"*, *"God bless the Prince of Wales"* and *"Now you've sunk the battleship"*. These catch-phrases are still remembered by his students today.

An excellent example of the memorable teaching style of Lockhart is given in a delightful little book, *Portraits from Memory*, by Sir James Howie. One passage in particular illustrates this well:

BODY LINES

Therefore, on my very first day in October 1925 at the University of Aberdeen, along with some half dozen other shrinking timid creatures from school, I went "down the Drain" to the practical anatomy classroom. This was, in fact, the dissecting room. Six dead bodies lay there under shrouds, stiff and cold. Notices on the wall assigned the novices to "arm" or "leg" on one of the six bodies. We hesitantly gathered round, wondering how we should ever venture to handle a dead body, let alone dissect it.

Into our midst breezed Robert Douglas Lockhart, an ex-Royal Navy officer, now lecturer in anatomy.

"Let's see now," he said. "You're not scared of dead bodies, are you? But you wonder how to begin." How right he was. "Let's get on with surface markings, then," he said. "You are on the arm. Run your hand over this ridge. That is the right clavicle or collar bone. On the left side is the other clavicle. See and feel the notch where they join the sternum or breast bone. Run your finger up towards the head from this notch till you meet an obstruction. That is the lower end of the larynx or voice box. Stop there. Just below that point, and at no other, you can save the life of a person choking to death from laryngeal obstruction – for example, from swallowing a fruit stone or from diphtheria affecting the larynx. Hold the trachea or windpipe steady, and stick in your knife just there. You'll have saved a life by doing an emergency tracheotomy to let in air. Nobody can do it who does not know his surface anatomy or carry a knife. There's no time to call the police, a doctor, or an ambulance. It's you and your knife – or nobody!" (Published by the British Medical Journal, 1988)

In his leisure time he was an enthusiastic cultivator of rhododendrons and produced several new varieties, one of which was named after his mother.

Professor Robert D Lockhart (1894-1987)

Professor Lockhart was an Honorary Member of the Society and left a large legacy for its benefit.

The portrait is by Sir James Gunn and was painted in 1965. Sir James Gunn was a Scot and was one of the great portrait painters of the twentieth century. An exhibition of his work was held in 1995 at the Fine Arts Society in London. The portrait was presented to Professor Lockhart by the University at a ceremony in the Mitchell Hall in 1965.

The portrait of his mother, by Alberto Morrocco, hangs beside his own by his request.

Professor Lockhart
and his rhododendrons

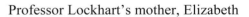
Professor Lockhart's mother, Elizabeth

BUSTS AND STATUETTES

Francis Adams

Sir James
McGrigor

Francis Adams (1796-1861)

(President of the Medico-Chirurgical Society, 1844)

Francis Adams was known as the most learned doctor in Britain. He was the son of a smallholder in the parish of Lumphanan, Aberdeenshire. He was educated at Aberdeen Grammar School and King's College, Aberdeen. After studying medicine for two years in Edinburgh and London, he set himself up as the first doctor in the village of Banchory, living in the Old Manse. He was President of the Society in 1844, having initially declined as he feared that distance would preclude proper attention to the duties of the post, and indeed he was rarely able to attend.

Dr Francis Adams

He was an outstanding example of the Victorian polymath. Besides being a devoted family man and a hard-working country doctor, he was a surgeon, medical scientist, ornithologist, botanist and poet. Largely self-taught, he became the leading classical scholar of his age and set himself the task of translating the corpus of medical knowledge from Greek, Roman and Arabic literature into English for the first time. This immense task he achieved by working in the early hours of the morning before he set off to work. His first publication was *"The Seven Books of Paulus Aegineta"*. This appeared in three volumes and was no simple translation; the original texts were accompanied by a commentary on the practices of the time and with references to the accepted medicine through the ages up to and including his own time. His later works were *"The Genuine Works of Hippocrates"* and *"The Extant Works of Aretaeus Cappodocean"*. These books are available in the Society's library.

He was offered the Chair of Greek at Aberdeen in 1827, and similar Chairs at other universities, but declined as he wished to continue in medical practice. He was awarded an Honorary LLD by Glasgow University in 1846, and a MD *honoris causa* by Aberdeen University in 1856. He also published medical papers on a variety of topics, ranging from adder bite to fatal rupture of aortic aneurysm in pregnancy.

He died in 1861 following pneumonia contracted after a night visit in dreadful weather to a sick patient.

The bust is the work of the sculptor, William Brodie, and was presented to the Society by Dr Adams' son, Dr Andrew Leith Adams. Originally a plumber's apprentice, Brodie's hobby was casting lead figures and medallion portraits of famous people. He later studied in Edinburgh and Rome, exhibited at the Royal Academy between 1846 and 1851, and was elected a member of the Royal Scottish Academy in 1859. His brother, Alexander, carved the statue of Queen Victoria which now stands at Queen's Cross, Aberdeen.

The bust was "lost" for a number of years, before being unearthed by Professor John Craig in 1951 under a table in a junk room in the old Brewery in King's College. The Society has recently had the bust of Dr Adams restored to its original state.

The Bust of
Dr Francis Adams
(1796-1861)

"the famous Grecian"
(hence the robes)

Alexander Kilgour (1803-1874)

(President of the Medico-Chirurgical Society, 1837 & 1852)

From humble beginnings, Dr Kilgour became the outstanding physician in Aberdeen and the North and had a national reputation. He was referred to as *"the Sydenham of the North"* by Dr John Brown, who, along with James Simpson and others, tried to entice him to Edinburgh. During his last illness he was attended by Lord Lister. He was active in university and hospital affairs and, in matters of public health, he introduced a registration of deaths in Aberdeen and campaigned vigorously for the establishment of a Fever Hospital. He was responsible for the founding of the Hospital for Incurables, later Morningfield Hospital, and gave his services to the hospital free. He was described as bluff and outspoken, with strong political opinions, although these changed over time.

In later life, he bought the small estate of Loirston at Cove and retired there. He provided a house for the first doctor in Cove, a Dr Ferguson, and a horse-drawn sledge, *"the horse being sharp-shod"*.

He was very active in affairs of the Society, first as Secretary to the junior members and later as President of the Society. He was also keen to protect the Society's library, and when it was being "misused", he suggested that Napoleon's words be placed above the door – *"Citizens, protect your own."* When he died, he left a substantial sum of money to the University. This money was used to found a Kilgour Chair of Geology and to provide a number of scholarships in natural science.

The bust was created by Joseph Whitehead and was given by Dr David Baird, Assistant Dean of the Medical Faculty in 1964. Other memorials are a medallion in the entrance to the old Infirmary at Woolmanhill, a portrait in the hospital archives, and Kilgour Avenue in Aberdeen.

Dr Alexander Kilgour (1803-1874)
(by permission of *NHS Grampian*)

The Bust of Dr Alexander Kilgour (1803-1874)

Alexander Harvey (1811-1889)

(President of the Medico-Chirurgical Society, 1864-65)

Alexander Harvey was the son of Dr Robert Harvey who was a founder member of the Society and President in 1818. He was born in 1811 and attended Aberdeen Grammar School and Marischal College. He then embarked on medical studies in Dublin, Paris, London and Edinburgh. In 1839, he was appointed Lecturer in physiology at Marischal College and Professor in the Practice of Medicine at King's College. In 1850, he resigned both posts and spent ten years in Southampton before returning to Aberdeen in 1860 to become the first Professor of Materia Medica in the combined universities. He resigned his chair in 1878 and died in London in 1889.

The bust appears to have been originally given to the University by Professor Harvey's son who was Director General of the Indian Medical Service. A Minute in 1982 states, *"We have also had passed into our keeping a bust of Professor Alexander Harvey of Aberdeen University. This bust, which had occupied various sites in the Medical School and was in danger of destruction during the recent and continuing alterations, has now been assured of a peaceful home".*

It seems likely that the sculptor was Joseph Whitehead, who was also responsible for the bust of Alexander Kilgour. Whitehead lived in Westminster and exhibited at the Royal Academy between 1889 and 1895. The bust of Harvey was produced in 1877 and that of Kilgour in 1895. Amongst his other subjects were George Stevenson and Lord Tennyson.

The Bust of Professor Alexander Harvey (1811-1889)

Sir James McGrigor

After his death, a large statue of Sir James McGrigor was erected at the headquarters of the Royal Army Medical College at Millbank in London. The Society's statue is a smaller copy. Originally in the possession of Aberdeen University, it was given for safe keeping to the Society by Dr G P Milne.

The Statue of Sir James McGrigor in the Royal Army Medical College, Millbank, London

The Statue of Sir James McGrigor

Charles Murray, CMG, LLD (1864-1941)

Charles Murray was described, during his lifetime, as *"The Chief Living Poet of Scotland"* by Neil Munro. His working life was spent in South Africa where he became Secretary for Public Works for the Union of South Africa, and he was involved in both the Boer War and the Great War. He retired to his birthplace in Alford, where he continued to write poetry in the local dialect. His best known work was *Hamewith and Other Poems*, published in 1927. He obviously had tremendous "presence", and was described as *"a raconteur of genius"*.

Although not a doctor, Charles Murray had many medical friends, including Sir Ashley Mackintosh, Professor McKerron, and the doctor poet, David Rorie. They, with others, formed a committee and at a ceremony in 1925, John Buchan, the writer and statesman (later Lord Tweedsmuir), presented him with a portrait by George Fiddes Watt, and his wife was presented with a bronze bust, now in Aberdeen Art Gallery. Our statuette is a smaller copy which belonged to Dr David Rorie and, on his death, it was given to Sir Alexander Greig Anderson, a prominent member of our Society. When he died, the statuette was presented to the Society by his niece, Miss Moira Anderson.

The bust is by Henry Snell Gambly, RSA, an Edinburgh sculptor who was responsible for a bust of Andrew Usher in the Usher Hall in Edinburgh. He also carved the medallions and decorative panels of that hall.

The Bust of Charles Murray (1864-1941)

MISCELLANEOUS TREASURES OF THE SOCIETY

The Painting of a Dissection

In 1794, the Society received a letter signed by six established medical practitioners, five of whom were founder members of the Society. They included James McGrigor. It contained the following passage: *"Above all we would recommend to the Society the study of anatomy. We are sorry that dissections have been so long neglected at Aberdeen. We are certain that proper subjects might be easily had there and will certainly be unless the students are wanting, to themselves, in spirited exertion or in common prudence. Bodies are procured in London for dissection almost every day. We leave everyone to form their own opinion whether it would not be an easier affair at Aberdeen."*

Before the receipt of this letter the students had dissected dogs, but even that practice had disappeared before the letter arrived. After a delay of a year or two the students followed the advice given, as a result of which mortsafes and watchtowers are today found in graveyards in Aberdeen and district. The acquiring of bodies for dissection, although officially forbidden, was unofficially condoned, as it was considered essential that students of medicine should have an adequate knowledge of anatomy. The painting of this dissection, as it is dated to the period when the practice of "body-snatching" was the only means in Aberdeen of obtaining bodies, is likely to have been that of a "subject".

The painting is reputed to be the work of James Giles, who studied anatomy at Marischal College and was friendly with the students of the Society. The painting is of high quality and has been dated to around 1820, which corresponds to the time that Giles would have been studying anatomy.

A second painting of a pelvis and lower limbs is in the possession of the Society but is of a much poorer quality.

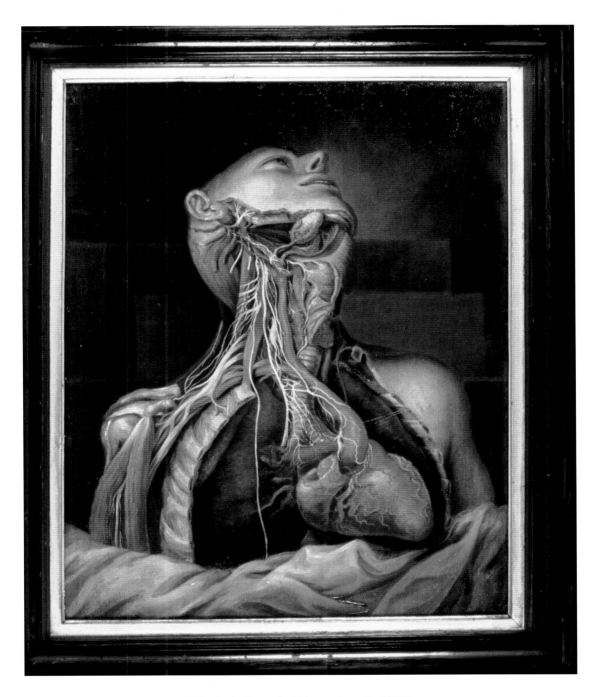

The Painting of a Dissection (*c.*1820)

Anatomical Drawings of Alberto Morrocco

Alberto Morrocco, RSA (1917-1998) was born in Aberdeen and, at the age of 14, entered Gray's School of Art in the city. He collaborated with Professor Lockhart in the Anatomy Department to produce the classic book by Lockhart, Hamilton and Fyfe, *The Anatomy of the Human Body*. These detailed studies were produced in 1949, and are in the Anatomy Collection of the University of Aberdeen, currently in Marischal College.

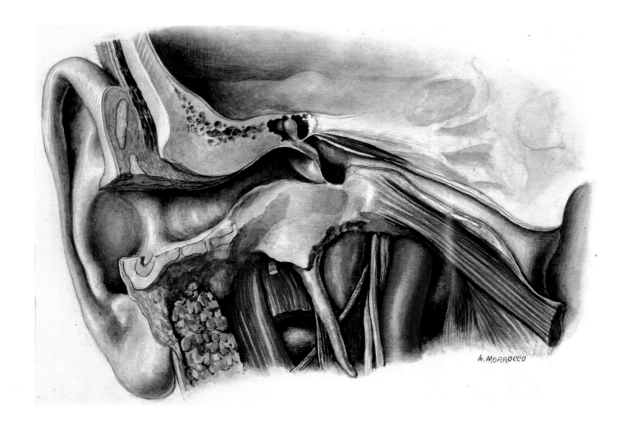

Anatomical Drawings of Alberto Morrocco (1949)
(by permission of the Department of Anatomy, University of Aberdeen)

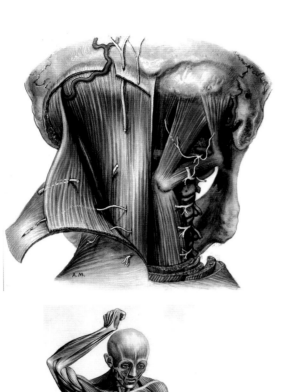

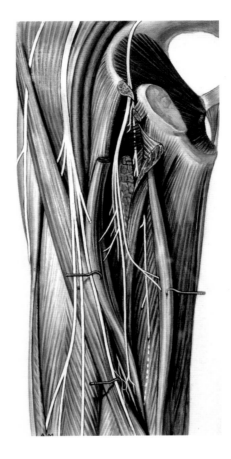

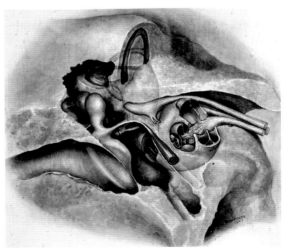

The Hogarth Cartoon

The Hogarth cartoon, originally entitled *"A company of undertakers"*, satirises physicians of his day. The faces at the top are those of well-known 'quack' doctors of the period. The other faces are those of contemporary physicians. They are smelling their canes, apart from two in the centre who are tasting urine, presumably for diabetes. Underneath is written the caption *"et plurima mortis imago"*.

The original cartoon was published in 1736. The framed cartoon in the Society's possession is a later copy dated 1809.

The Hogarth Cartoon

The Chalmers Cartoon

The Chalmers Cartoon is of Professor William Chalmers, MD, Mediciner (Professor of Medicine), King's College, 1782-1792. The cartoon was presented to the Society by his great-great-grandson, Rev James Smith, BD, Minister of St George's and the West, Aberdeen.

The cartoon is taken from one of Kay's portraits. It is entitled *"The Sapient Septemviri"* and shows the seven opponents in 1786 to the plan for the union of King's and Marischal Colleges. In the original portrait, the caption for Professor Chalmers reads, *"Degrees, male and female in medicine and midwifery sold here for ready money"*.

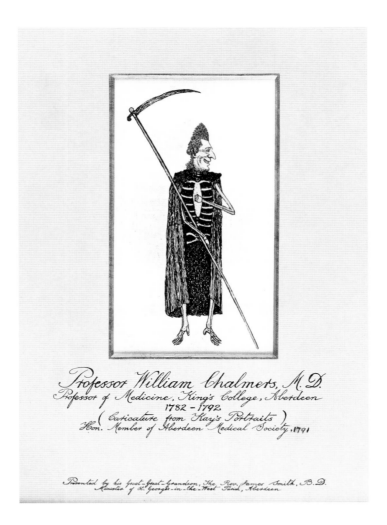

The Chalmers Cartoon

The Etching of Hippocrates

The etching of a marble bust of Hippocrates is entitled *"Hippocrates Heraclidae"*. Underneath is inscribed, *"He grounded his precepts upon Æsculapius. He was, by some, styled the Prince of Physicians and, by others, honoured as a god, and his works are to this* *day greatly esteemed in most parts of Europe. He dyed* (sic) *at 104 years of age about 425 years before the birth of Christ."*

The etching is undated but is probably eighteenth century.

HIPPOCRATES HIRACLIDÆ F. CO'S.

The Etching of Hippocrates

The Death Mask of Napoleon

This death mask was found by Dr Reid while he was Lecturer in Anatomy in London. An Aberdeen graduate, he was later Professor of Anatomy in Aberdeen. The death mask was found under a seat, and he brought it back with him to Aberdeen to the Anatomy Museum and it has since been passed on to our collection. Alongside the death mask is a framed copy of the post-mortem report on Napoleon, with the five signatories. One of these is Charles Mitchell, MD, an Aberdeen graduate who was called into consultation on Napoleon shortly before his death. Another Aberdeen graduate, Dr Patrick Blaikie, accompanied Napoleon on the *Bellerophon* on his final voyage to St. Helena. Dr Blaikie was the Surgeon on board and, on leaving the Navy, he became Lecturer on Anatomy and Surgery in Aberdeen, where he was very well regarded. He was President of the Medico-Chirurgical Society in 1823.

There is a collection of papers relating to the death mask in the archives.

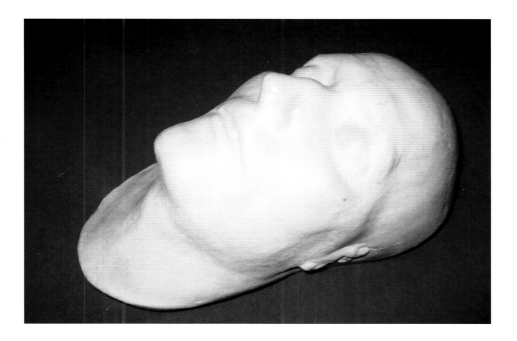

The Death Mask of Napoleon

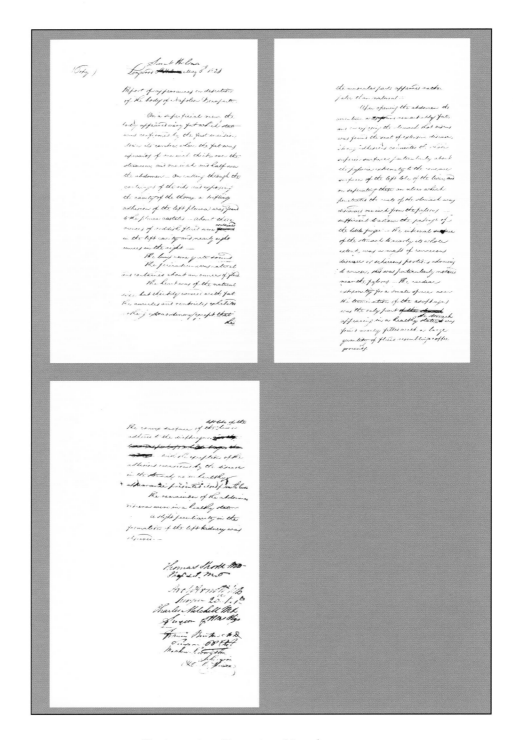

Post-mortem Report on Napoleon

Transcription of the post-mortem report on Napoleon with the five signatories:

Longwood Saint Helena May 8th 1821

Report of the appearances on desection of the body of Napoleon Bonaparte.

  On a superficial view the body appeared very fat which state was confirmed by the first incision down the centre where the fat was upwards of an inch thick over the sternum, and one inch and a half over the abdomen— On cutting through the cartilages of the ribs and exposing the cavity of the thorax a trifling adhesion of the left pleura was found to the pleura costalis—about three ounces of reddish fluid were contained in the left cavity and nearly eight ounces in the right.—
The lungs were quite sound
The pericardium was natural and contained about an ounce of fluid
The heart was of the natural size but thickly covered with fat. The auricles and ventricles exhibited nothing extraordinary except that the muscular parts appeared rather paler than natural. Upon opening the abdomen the omentum was found remarkably fat. And on exposing the stomach that viscus was found the seat of extensive disease, strong adhesions connected the whole superior surface particularly about the pyloric extremity to the concave surface of the left lobe of the liver, and on separating these an ulcer which penetrated the coats of the stomach was discovered one inch from the pylorus---sufficient to allow the passage of the little finger—the internal surface of the stomach to almost its whole extent, was a mass of cancerous disease and scirrhous portions advancing to cancer, this was particularly noticed near the pylorus—The cardiac extremity for a small space near the termination of the oesophagus was the only part appearing in a healthy state, the stomach was found nearly filled with a large quantity of fluid resembling coffee grounds.
  The convex surface of the left lobe of the liver adhered to the diaphragm. With the exception of the adhesions occasioned by the disease in the stomach no unhealthy appearance presented itself in the liver.
  The remainder of the abdominal viscera were in a healthy state.
  A slight peculiarity in the formation of the left kidney was observed.

Thomas Shortt MD
Arch Arnott MD
Charles Mitchell MD
Thomas Burton MD
Matthew Livingston
Surgeon

The Engraved Plate of the Society

The engraved plate is in the style of the early nineteenth century. Under the arched heading *'Medico-Chirurgical Society, Aberdeen'*, it shows a Genius entering from the left. In his right hand he holds the torch of life, and protects the flame with his left. At no great distance from his feet lies a skull showing the course of man's mortal life. Behind the Genius there is a small conventional rosebush. On the right is an open volume displaying anatomical study. The book is titled *Anatomy*, and the open page displays a drawing of a skeleton. Across the book lies the rod and serpent of Æsculapius, and a bush of bay laurel completes the picture.

The plate was used for printing cards of invitation and certificates of performance.

The Engraved Plate of the Society

The Seal of the Society

The Seal of the Society shows Hippocrates with his name in Greek characters, encircled by *"Sigillum Societat.: Med.chir.: Abredonensis"*.

At the meeting of the Society on 14 January 1791, several designs and mottos were laid before the Society to choose from, amongst them one to be engraved on copper, and an impression given to every member who has been one full year in the Society. The design chosen was the head of Hippocrates within a circle *"1789. Aberdoniae Medicae Institutae"* and below the motto *"Res Medica Floreat"*. The head of Hippocrates, as described above, became the seal of the Society, and *"Res Medica Floreat"* its motto. On the title page of Volume 2 of the Minutes appears the motto, *"Concordia Res Parvae Crescunt"*. This came to be used, along with *"Res Medica Floreat"*, as a second motto of the Society.

The Seal of the Society

The Presidential Medallion

The medallion is of gold. Down the centre is a tapered rod (the rod of Æsculapius) surmounted by a castle representing the City of Aberdeen. Around the rod is entwined the snake of Æsculapius. The rod and castle are of white gold, set against the yellow gold of the medallion itself. On each side of the rod, in relief, are carved two leopards, again representing the City of Aberdeen. On the back of the medallion is inscribed *'Aberdeen Medico-Chirurgical Society'*.

The medallion was commissioned by the Society on the occasion of its bicentenary in 1989, and was crafted by Malcolm Appleby. He was born in 1946 and studied at the Central School of Art and the Royal College of Art in London before establishing his studio near Banchory, where he practised as a silversmith and metal engraver. He is known for his imaginative use of materials, and his work is exhibited in the National Museums of Scotland, Aberdeen Art Gallery and Museums, and the Victoria and Albert Museum.

The
Presidential
Medallion

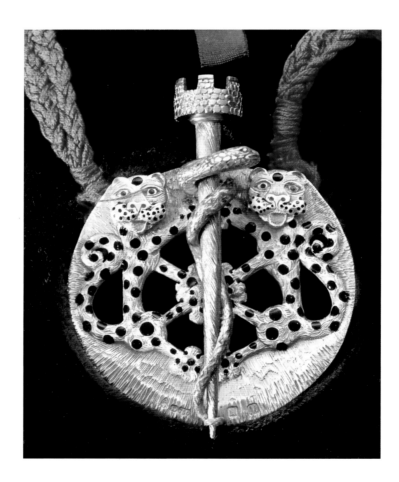

The Presidential Gown

The Presidential gown was presented to the Society by Professor Sir Ashley Mackintosh. It is black with gold trimming and bears, on opposite lapels, the seal and the emblem of the Society linked by a gold chain.

A Minute of the meeting of 18th November, 1920 reads, *"A letter from the President was read suggesting that an official gown might be provided for the President of the Society and if this proposal met with approval, he was willing to defray the cost"*. However, it was not until the annual dinner in 1927 that the gown was available. It is noted, *"A feature of the evening was the wearing by the President of the new Presidential Gown"*.

The Presidential Gown and Medallion

(Dr Marion White, President 2007-08)

The Ashley Mackintosh Golf Cup

In 1920, his presidential year, Professor Sir Ashley Mackintosh presented a cup for competition by members of the Society. He proposed that an annual golf competition, confined to members of the Society, be held and suggested that the play should be of a foursome character. Since then the silver cup has been presented to the winners of the competition at the annual dinner, usually (at least latterly) with a tongue-in-cheek speech declaiming the golfing prowess of the winners.

The Ashley Mackintosh Golf Cup

The Silver Candlesticks

Two silver candlesticks were presented to the Society in 1989 to mark the bicentenary of the Society. They are inscribed *'Presented by Forfarshire Medical Society to Aberdeen* *Medico-Chirurgical Society on the occasion of its bicentenary'*. They grace the top table at the Society's annual Founder's Dinner.

The silver candlesticks

Hugo Rheinhold's *'Monkey contemplating a human skull'*

The bronze statuette of a monkey contemplating a human skull is one of the most interesting articles in our collection. It shows a chimpanzee sitting on a pile of books and contemplating a human skull, which is held in the animal's right hand. The left hand is holding its jaw, and the right foot holds a pair of dividers. One of the pile of books is lettered *'Darwin'* on its spine, and on another is the inscription *"Eritis sicut deus"*, taken from the book of Genesis.

The statue was created by Hugo Rheinhold and was first shown at the great Berlin Art Exhibition in 1892. Eight statuettes were cast from the mould; the one in possession of our Society was given by Dr David Rorie, in his will in 1946. Dr Rorie had bought the statuette when he visited Berlin just before the First World War. Another cast stands prominently on the desk used by Lenin in the Kremlin, given as a gift by Armand Hammer who bought it in London on his way to visit the Russian leader in 1922. Hammer was a Russian émigré with a great love of his native land. He rose to prominence, and controversy, in international business.

The sculpture continues to attract a global audience, and numerous copies have been made, particularly in America and Germany.

'Monkey contemplating a human skull' by Hugo Rheinhold (1892)

Silver Medal in the Practice of Medicine

The Silver Medal was awarded to William Pirie in 1894; it was superseded the following year by the Anderson Gold Medal.

James Anderson, MA, MB CM, MD, FRCP (1853-1893), graduated with honours in medicine. He was lecturer in pathology at the London Hospital when he died. The Anderson Gold Medal and Prize was founded in his memory from funds raised by public subscription.

Silver Medal in the Practice of Medicine

The Keith Gold Medal

The Keith Gold Medal was founded in 1881 by Major George Keith, in memory of his father, the late William Keith, MD, Surgeon in the Royal Infirmary at Aberdeen.

William Keith was well known as a speedy and skilful lithotomist, at a time when *"cutting for stone"* was one of the few recognised operations in pre-anaesthetic days. He obviously had the surgeon's approach to his work and his results, as shown by an entry in the Minutes of the Society from 1843. He is describing his results of operations for stone, of which 20 were cured and 2 died, *"... one died from an injury done by the night nurse, and the other from overbleeding from leech bites."* It is interesting that, even then, post-operative mortality was never the surgeon's fault. However, there is no doubt that these are outstanding results from an exceptional surgeon, and reflect his dedication to post-operative care.

The medal is awarded annually after the examination in systematic and clinical surgery. The medal in the possession of the Society was awarded to Janet C Nichol in 1921.

The Keith
Gold Medal

Bladder stones
(from the Society's collection; the larger measures 7 cm across)

The Shepherd Memorial Gold Medal

A second medal, The Shepherd Memorial Gold Medal, is awarded annually after examination on the principles and practice of surgery. Surgeon Major Peter Shepherd, a local man, graduated MB at Aberdeen in 1864. From 1872 he was attached to the military hospital in Woolwich. While there, he gave the first lectures on first-aid in 1878, and he is recognised as the founder of *First-Aid*. The lectures were an immediate success and were collected by Shepherd into a booklet, which was published after his death in 1879 by his friend, Sir James Cantlie.

The concept of first-aid was an immediate success; within a few years, many thousands of his books were sold, and first-aid was taught in four continents.

Surgeon Major Shepherd was killed at the battle of Isandhlwana in 1879 and, in his memory, his colleagues collected money for the establishment of the gold medal award.

First-Aid Book

Surgeon Major Peter Shepherd

The Cigarette Card Album

The album contains a complete set of cigarette cards on the subject of first-aid, dated to the First World War. It was produced by Sir James Cantlie, who was closely involved with Dr

Shepherd in establishing the new discipline of first-aid. The album was presented to the Society by its former librarian, Dr Ian Porter.

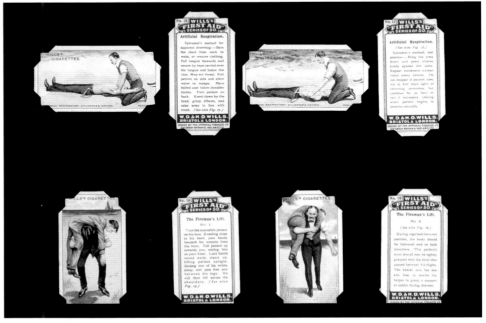

Dr Esslemont's CBE

(President of the Medico-Chirurgical Society, 1957-58)

Mary Esslemont (1891-1984) was a GP in Aberdeen for 30 years and was a pioneer in women's medicine in many fields. She served on numerous committees, including Public Health, Joint BMA and Royal College of Nursing, and was the first woman to serve on the Scottish Council of the BMA, becoming its chairman in 1968. She was the first woman assessor on the University Court.

For her many achievements, she was awarded the CBE in 1955 and the Freedom of the City of Aberdeen in 1981 - a very rare honour.

Dr Mary
Esslemont

Dr Esslemont's
CBE

Medical Women's Federation Medallion

This jewelled medallion was presented to the Aberdeen Medical Women's Federation by Dr Mary Esslemont in 1965. Due to social change the Federation was wound up, and the medallion was given to the Society for safe-keeping.

Medical Women's Federation Medallion

The Grandfather Clock

The grandfather clock stands at the end of the corridor. It is described as *'a tall eight-day clock in inlaid mahogany case with brass and silver dial by William Spark, Aberdeen, presented by Dr J F Christie, 1927'*. Dr Christie was President of the Society in 1926.

William Spark was an eminent clock maker whose business is listed as having been in Marischal Street in 1820. The clock required several repairs as recorded in the Building Officer's Report of 1977. Since then, however it has continued to give good service and keeps accurate time.

The grandfather clock

The Lectern

The lectern is described as *"mahogany lectern on fluted pedestal support"*. It was presented to the Society in 1936 by Dr John Johnston, who was President in that year. Dr Johnston was a General Practitioner in Aberdeen and Anaesthetist at the Infirmary. He was an authority on local history, a Fellow of the Society of Antiquaries and was one of fourteen founder members of the Scottish Society of Anaesthetists inaugurated in February 1914, the oldest Anaesthetic Society in Britain.

The lectern

The Ballot Boxes

The Regulations of the Society (Minute Book 1, 1789) record:

> *18. That the admission of new as well as the expulsion of offending members shall be determined by Ballot.*

The original box was a simple affair with leather hinges and a single aperture. The second ballot box is a tapered wooden box, and white balls were inserted through the "Yes" hole to support a motion, and black balls were put through the "No" hole to indicate rejection, although some members have been known to habitually "black ball" individuals out of a sense of mischief rather than for any good reason; such votes were usually ignored.

In the early days of the Society, admission was by a rigorous examination conducted by the Board of Examiners drawn from the membership of the Society. A candidate had to be vouched for by the doctor to whom he was apprenticed. He had to translate a few sentences in Latin and then pass an examination in Anatomy and Physiology, and sometimes in Surgery and Chemistry.

The ballot boxes

The McGrigor Centenary Plaque

The plaque was presented to the Society by the Director-General of the Army Medical Services at a reception to celebrate the centenary in 1958 of the death of Sir James McGrigor. It features the badges of the Royal Army Medical Corps, the Royal Army Dental Corps and the Queen Alexandra's Imperial Military Nursing Service, called at that time (as per the badge shown below) the Queen Alexandra's Royal Army Nursing Corps.

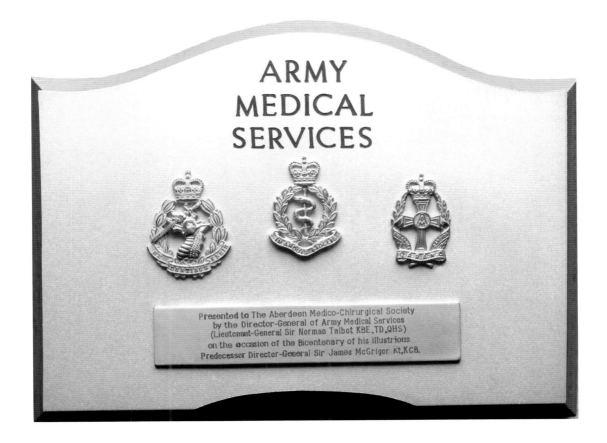

The McGrigor Centenary Plaque

The War Memorial Plaque

The war memorial plaque, commemorating those members of the Society who lost their lives whilst serving the armed forces in two world wars, was designed by Dr William Kelly, an Aberdeen architect. The plaque was purchased by subscription.

The names on the plaque are:

Clifford Thiselton Bell, Captain RAMC, graduated in 1896. He was assistant Medical Electrician at the Infirmary and Senior Medical Officer at Old Mill, which was taken over as a hospital during the war. He died in the 1st Scottish General Hospital, Aberdeen in 1919.

Arthur Kellas, Major RAMC. He was Senior Assistant at the Royal Asylum, Aberdeen before the war. He was killed in the Gallipoli campaign in 1915 while inspecting his company of the 1st Highland Field Ambulance before an impending battle.

Arthur Hugh Lister, Captain RAMC, was Lord Lister's nephew. After graduating BA in Cambridge he studied medicine at Aberdeen, graduating in 1895 with the highest honours. He became physician to the Royal Infirmary and Lecturer in Clinical Medicine, and had a large practice in Aberdeen. In 1906, he presented a comprehensive scheme for dealing with pulmonary tuberculosis among the poor of Aberdeen. Whilst serving as Commander of the 19th General Hospital in Alexandria he became ill, having never been in robust health, and was being invalided home when he died at sea in 1916. He had the reputation of being a very hard worker, not considering his own health, and was clearly very popular with, and admired by, both his colleagues and his patients. There is a memorial to him, erected by his widow, in St. Margaret's Church in the Spital in Aberdeen.

Joseph Ellis Milne, Captain RAMC. He served as a Medical Officer and was awarded the DSO for his work at the Battle of the Somme (*"For conspicuous gallantry and devotion to duty during operations. He has repeatedly tended the wounded under heavy shell fire, and has shown himself utterly regardless of personal safety."*). He was killed in action at Ypres in 1917.

James Dickson Noble, Captain RAMC. He was accidentally killed at Aberdeen in 1914.

James Robertson, Lieutenant Colonel RAMC. He was educated at Robert Gordon's College and Aberdeen University, and was clearly a "high-flyer", having subsequently studied and worked in London, Dublin and Berlin. He was a Senior Assistant Anaesthetist at the Royal Infirmary when he joined the RAMC in 1914. He was rapidly promoted and in 1918, when he was killed at Bapaume, he was the Commanding Officer of the 2nd/1st Highland Field Ambulance.

Cuthbert Alexander Cromar, Captain RAMC, was lost at sea in 1942. He was a well respected General Practitioner in Torry when war broke out and, as a Territorial, he was mobilised. His name was added after World War II.

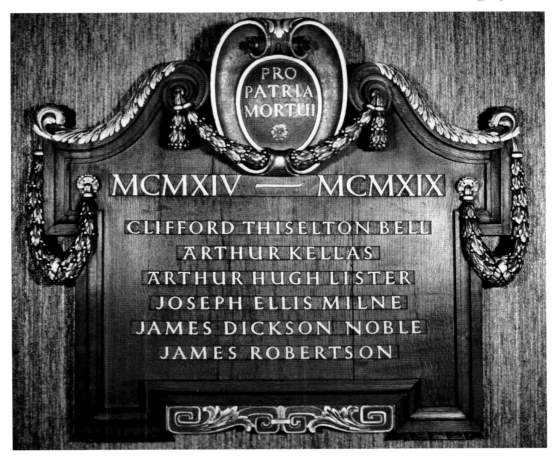

PRO
PATRIA
MORTUI

MCMXIV — MCMXIX

CLIFFORD THISELTON BELL
ARTHUR KELLAS
ARTHUR HUGH LISTER
JOSEPH ELLIS MILNE
JAMES DICKSON NOBLE
JAMES ROBERTSON

The War Memorial Plaque

Top row (L to R)
C Cromar, J Robertson,
A Kellas

Bottom row (L to R)
C Bell, J Noble, A H Lister,
J E Milne

The King Street Hall

In its early years, the Society met in several places, including at one time, the Professor of Greek's classroom. A Minute in 1806 reads, *"Dr McGrigor was the first to suggest erection of a Hall and subscribed fifty guineas. Dr McGrigor has all along manifested himself as the Society's best benefactor and warmest friend"*. A subscription list was opened in Aberdeen, Edinburgh and London newspapers, but money was slow in coming in. Eventually, a feu in King Street was purchased from the Town Council, and in 1820 the Society's building was completed to the designs of the noted architect, Archibald Simpson. In the building was accommodated the Society's Library and Museum, and it was the meeting place of the Society from 1820 to 1973.

The Meeting Hall in the King Street building

The King Street Hall

The Subscription List

A framed list of subscribers to the King Street building is displayed in the Society's hall. McGrigor was the largest donor. The list was found in the attic of the King Street building at the time of the removal to Foresterhill. It was cleaned and framed before being mounted in the corridor of the Society's hall.

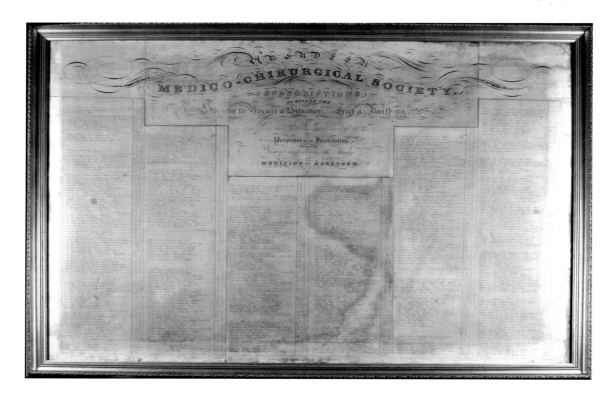

The Subscription List

The Foresterhill Building

By the 1960s, the hall in King Street had become increasingly inconvenient for the meetings of the Society, and discussions were begun to build a site at Foresterhill. In 1967, in agreement with the University, a plan for a building on the Foresterhill site was adopted. By 1971, the secretary was indicating in the annual report of Council that the new building was continuing to rise and, in 1973, the move from King Street to Foresterhill was completed. The move was commemorated by a plaque in the Society's hall, which reads: *"Aberdeen Medico-Chirurgical Society founded 1789. This building at Foresterhill was opened by Principal Edward M Wright, 9th April, 1973".*

The Medico-Chirurgical Society's Hall at Foresterhill

The Hall in the Medico-Chirurgical Society's Building at Foresterhill

(showing the dominating portraits of Sir Alexander Ogston on the left, and Sir James McGrigor on the right; photographed at Dr Melvin Morrison's Presidential Address, June 2007)

The Council Chamber in the Medico-Chirurgical Society's Building at Foresterhill

*(showing the bust of Francis Adams on the left, and the library on the right;
and the portraits of Sir Ashley Mackintosh on the left and Sir John Marnoch on the right)*

The Plane Tree

Outside the entrance to the Society's hall stands a large and flourishing plane tree. A plaque near the base of the tree reads: *"This plane tree* *grew from a seed of the plane tree in the island of KOS under which Hippocrates taught his students. A gift from Dr Alistair Forbes."*

The Plane Tree

The Plane Tree
plaque

The Presidential Chair

The Presidential Chair was gifted to the Society by Sir James McGrigor. A minute of a meeting in 1821 recorded that *"the President's Committee acknowledge the receipt of a superb chair, presented to the Society by James McGrigor, for the use of the President"*.

It is a stately piece of furniture, upholstered in red leather, the arms supported in front by winged lions, which extend downwards as the front legs to end in clawed feet. The design is typical of the Empire style, which originated in Paris after the Revolution, and was called the Regency style in England.

The
Presidential
Chair

The Members' Chairs

In 1821, each member of the Society presented a chair. These were described as *"mahogany stuffed chairs for the large hall"*, and are still in use. All fifty of the original chairs were repaired in 1976 and renovation of the chairs was carried out in 1987.

A Member's Chair

The Junior Members' President's Chair

The Presidential Chair for the Junior (Second) Class was presented by Harry Leith Lumsden, the Laird of Clova and Auchindoir *"in lieu of his subscription of five guineas"* in 1823.

The Junior Members' President's Chair

The Kayak

Our Kayak hanging in the corridor attracts more attention than any other single item in the collection. The kayak is a small, light, strong, manoeuvrable boat which is virtually unsinkable. By its speed and silence, it enabled Eskimos to hunt seals, walruses and whales, and was essential for their survival.

In 1839, Eenoolooapik, an Eskimo from Baffin Land, was brought to Aberdeen by Captain Penny in his whaling ship. Eenoolooapik demonstrated his skill with the kayak on the River Dee, including in his repertoire the *"Eskimo roll"*. Afterwards, he fell ill and was treated by William Pirrie, Professor of Surgery. He recovered and returned to his home in 1840. It is believed, though there is no proof, that Eenoolooapik gave his kayak to Professor Pirrie in recognition of his treatment and that Professor Pirrie gave it, in turn, to our Society. The kayak, in very good condition, has excited much interest amongst visitors from Canada and USA.

As there is no wood in Baffin Land, the kayak is made of sealskin and bone, and is beautifully constructed. There are a few small pieces of driftwood in the framework around the seat in the kayak. The central cockpit has a collar, around which the occupant's anorak can be sealed, forming a single watertight unit. Several tears in the hull had been carefully repaired by the owner. Our boat is in an excellent state of preservation; two others, in poor condition, are in the Marischal Museum.

Professor William Pirrie
Regius Professor of Surgery

(known by his students as "The Barron", with two "r"s, to acknowledge his spelling of Pirrie, and his fondness of describing his teaching by Baron Dupuytren in Paris.

President of the Medico-Chirurgical Society, 1872)

Drawing of Eenoolooapik

The Kayak

The Library

The library was established in 1791 with three books (Sydenham's *Opera*, Salmon's *Ars Chirurgica* and Graham's *Physiological Essays*). It rapidly grew and, until the beginning of the 20th century, it was one of the great medical collections with over 10,000 volumes, 2,000 theses (including 300 theses from the Dutch universities 1654-1780) and 3,000 pamphlets and periodicals. The oldest book was *The Works of Albert di Villa Nova* (1533). However, by the 1960s it was little used and it was decided to sell the library to acquire funds to build the new hall at Foresterhill. Books and papers of local interest were retained and formed the nucleus of a new library devoted to medical history, with particular reference to Aberdeen and the north of Scotland. In addition to books, manuscripts and other documents, there is a growing collection of medical instruments dating back to 1798.

A few of the library's treasures are illustrated.

The Library in the King Street Hall

The Students' Notes

The library contains many volumes of notes taken by medical students from 1776 onwards.

The Junior Members of this Society recorded presentations which were considered to be of a high standard in a series of volumes called *"Thesauri"*. These demonstrate the medical teaching of the time, much of which was based on the works of Cullen, the leading physician of his day.

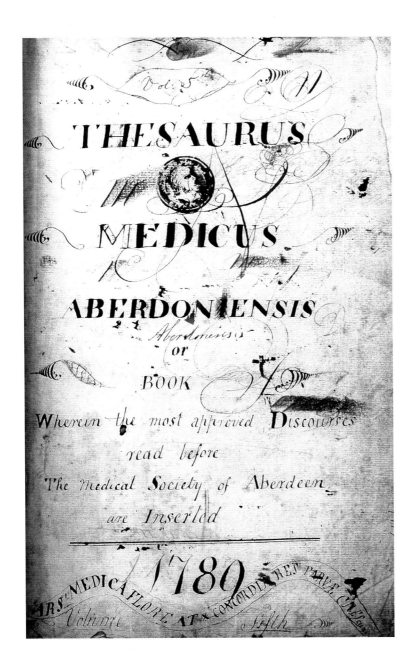

The Students' notes

Minute Books

Frontispiece of the first Minute Book (1789)

The library contains a complete set of the minutes of the Junior and Senior Sections of the Society, dating from 1789. They provide a fascinating insight into the medical world through the centuries. The entries tend to be short and factual, with an occasional lighter note. For instance, after the election of James Robertson as the first Secretary (contested also by John Grant) on 15th October, 1790, *"We then proceeded to the Tavern, where we spent the greater Part of the Meeting in Mirth and Jollity."* (Was this the first Founder's Dinner?)

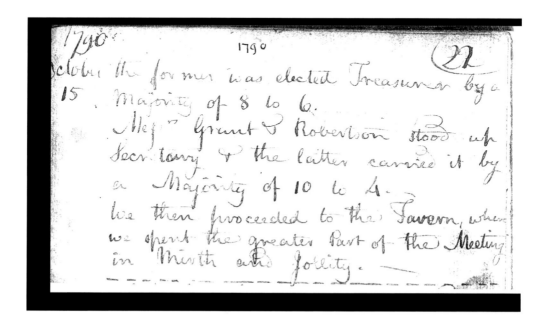

The Minute Books also record the subjects of debate to be *"agitated"* by the members at their meetings. Some of these are still the subject of controversy today, some 200 years later.

For example, it is noted, in James McGrigor's handwriting on January 5th, 1790, *"Is an accurate knowledge of Anatomy absolutely necessary to Medicine?"*

In 1795, the treatment of cancer of the breast was debated, including the use of live toads, which one member stated *"in several instances had been found of service."*

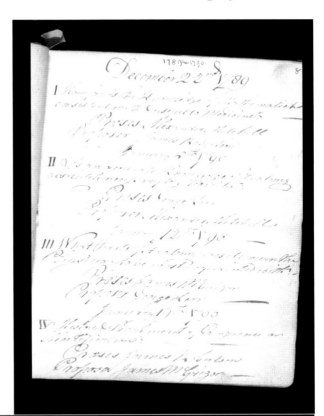

The Minute Books of the Society, recording the topics discussed 1789-90

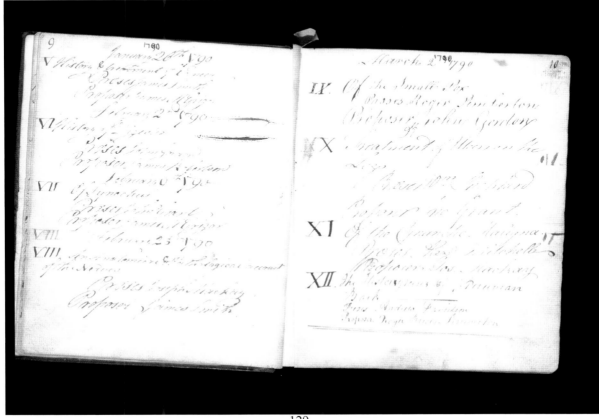

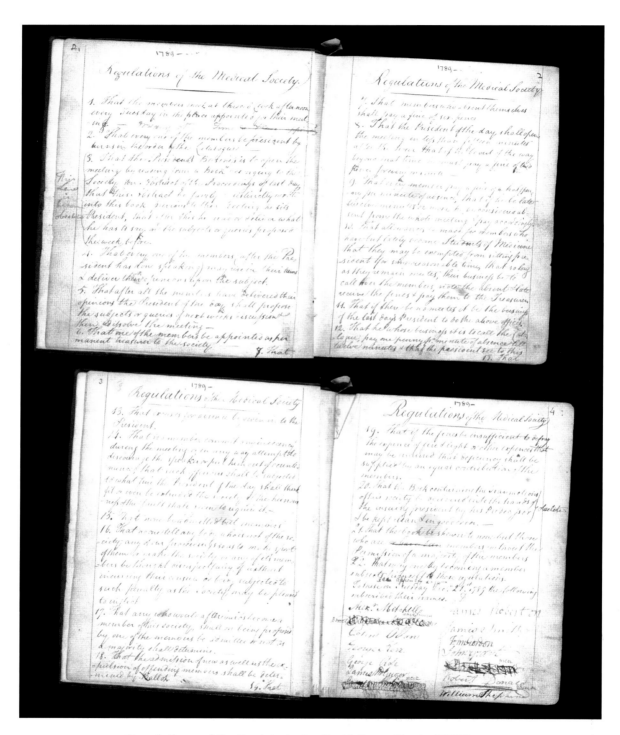

Regulations of the Society in the first Minute Book (1789)

Transcription of the Regulations of the Society in the first Minute Book (1789):

1789 – Regulations of the Medical Society

1.   *That the members meet at three o'clock afternoon every Tuesday in the place appointed for their meeting. Or at any other time.*
2.   *That every one of the members be president by turns in the order of the catalogue.*
3.   *That the President's Business is to open the meeting by reading from a Book belonging to the Society an Abstract of the Proceedings of last day, that this Abstract be fairly and distinctly wrote into this book previous to the meeting he sits President, that after this he read or deliver what he has to say on the subjects or queries proposed the week before.*
4.   *That every one of the members (after the President has done speaking) may rise in their turns and deliver their opinions upon the subject.*
5.   *That after all the members have delivered their opinions, the President of the day shall propose the subjects or queries of next weeks discussion and then dissolve the meeting.*
6.   *That one of the members be appointed as permanent treasurer to the Society.*
7.   *That the members who absent themselves shall pay a fine of sixpence.*
8.   *That the President of the day shall open the meeting in less than fifteen minutes after the hour, that if he be out of the way beyond that time he must pay a fine of twopence for every minute.*
9.   *That every member pay a fine of a half penny per minute of absence, that if he be late twelve minutes or more he be considered absent from the whole meeting and pay accordingly.*
10.   *That allowance be made for members who have but lately became Students of Medicine that they may be exempted from sitting president for some reasonable time, that so long as they remain mutes, their business be to call over the members, note the absent and late, receive the fines and pay them to the Treasurer.*
11.   *That if there be no mutes, it be the business of the last day's president to do the above offices.*
12.   *That he whose business it is to call the catalogue, pay one penny pr. minute of absence till twelve minutes and that the president see to this.*
13.   *That excuses for absence be given in to the President.*
14.   *That no member commit any indecency during the meeting or in any way attempt to discourage the speaker or put him out of countenance, that such offenders shall be subjected to what fine the President of the day shall think fit or even be extruded the society if the heinousness of the fault shall seem to require it.*
15.   *That none be admitted but members.*
16.   *That no one tell anybody who is not of the society any of our proceedings so as to make sport of them or make the society or any of it's members be thought disrespectfully of without incurring their censure or being subjected to such penalty as the Society may be pleased to inflict.*
17.   *That any who would afterwards become a member of this society, shall on being proposed by one of the members be admitted or not as a majority shall determine.*
18.   *That the admission of new as well as the expulsion of offending members shall be determined by Ballot.*
19.   *That if the fines be insufficient to defray the expense of fire and light or other expenses that may be incurred that deficiency shall be supplied by an equal contribution of the members.*
20.   *That the book containing the Transactions of this society be delivered into the hands of the ensuing president by his predecessor and be kept clean and in good order. (Obsolete)*
21.   *That the book be shewn to none but those who are members without the permission of a majority of the members.*
22.   *That everyone by becoming a member subjects himself to these regulations.*

Certificate awarded to Junior Members of the Society

In 1789, the founders of the original Society were all undergraduates. After the Medico-Chirurgical Society was re-constituted in 1812, there were two sections, First and Second: the "Senior" members were the qualified doctors, and the "Junior" members were the medical students. The Junior Section had its own President and Secretary, and met in the Library of the King Street Hall. The Junior Section took it upon themselves to agitate for improvements in medical teaching, and, as they gradually succeeded, the need for their existence diminished, to be replaced eventually by the University Medical Society.

Certificate awarded to Junior Members of the Society

Certificate awarded to the winner of the Strachan Bursary

Funds for the Strachan Bursary were left in a legacy of Mr William Strachan of Moreseat, who had been Headmaster of Robert Gordon's College. In his will, it is stated that the legacy is for *"the purpose of funding a medical bursary or bursaries in Aberdeen, said bursary or bursaries to be under the control and management of a Council of the Aberdeen Medico-Chirurgical Society"*.

Certificate awarded to the winner of the Strachan Bursary

The Med-Chi Student Elective Bursaries and the Adam Quaich

Five bursaries, of £500 each, are awarded annually for the best Final Year Medical Student Elective projects. The eponymous names associated with these awards are taken from renowned Aberdonian pioneers in medicine, all of whom feature elsewhere in this book: Sir James MacGrigor, Sir Ashley Mackintosh, Sir Patrick Manson, Professor Hans Kosterlitz and Professor John Mallard.

The recipients of these awards are expected to make a short presentation about their Elective project at a meeting of the Society, usually in October each year. The best presentation is awarded the Adam Quaich, named in honour of Mr Alexander Adam (Honorary Librarian of the Society since 1983) and first presented in 1998.

The Adam Quaich

The McGrigor Archives

In 1847, Sir James McGrigor sent to the Society his collection of medical records from the beginning of his military service until the end of the Peninsular War in 1814, with a covering letter.

The McGrigor Archives consist of over 60 volumes of manuscript, and include returns of wounded and diseased soldiers throughout his service as Regimental Surgeon, and from his staff during the Peninsular War. Also included are 15 handwritten volumes of his personal journal of his experiences in the Peninsula. Altogether they form a unique source of military history of the period.

Transcript of the letter from McGrigor to the Society in 1847:

London 4th August 1847

Sir
*   I send by the ship*
*   Volumes of Manuscripts being chiefly cases of Disease which occurred in the Regimental Hospital of the 88th Regiment and of the Royal Regiment of Horse Guards when I was Surgeon of these Corps and subsequently when I was on the Medical Staff of the Army and which I beg you to present in my name to the Medical Society of Aberdeen. In presenting these Volumes I do so not on account of their value which I am very sensible is but small but as holding out to the Junior Members of the Society an instance of the persevering industry with which I prosecuted my profession from my first entrance into the army and to which I mainly attribute my success in it. The Clinical Cases are mainly in my own hand writing but sometimes in that of my assistants in the two regiments in which I served as Surgeon viz. nearly 11 years in the 88th Regt. and about two years in the Royal Regiment of Horse Guards. My assistants were*
*   Mr Thom of Aberdeen*
*   Mr Ninian Bruce of do.*
*   Mr Peter Nicol of do.*
*   Dr Jno. Brown of Skene Square Aberdeen*
*   Dr Laing of Golden Sq. Aberdeen*
*   Mr Tonera of Ireland*
*   and*
*   Mr Peach of Somersetshire.*

I was I believe the Institutor of the Medical Society of Aberdeen for after my return from Edinburgh where I had been a Member of the Medical and Chirurgical Society in a conversation with the late Dr James Robertson I suggested such an Institution as I had been a member of in Edinburgh and a short time after the Society commenced its Sittings. With my warmest wishes for its prosperity.
*   I have the honor to be*
*   Sir*
*   Your Most Obedient Servant*
*   J McGrigor*

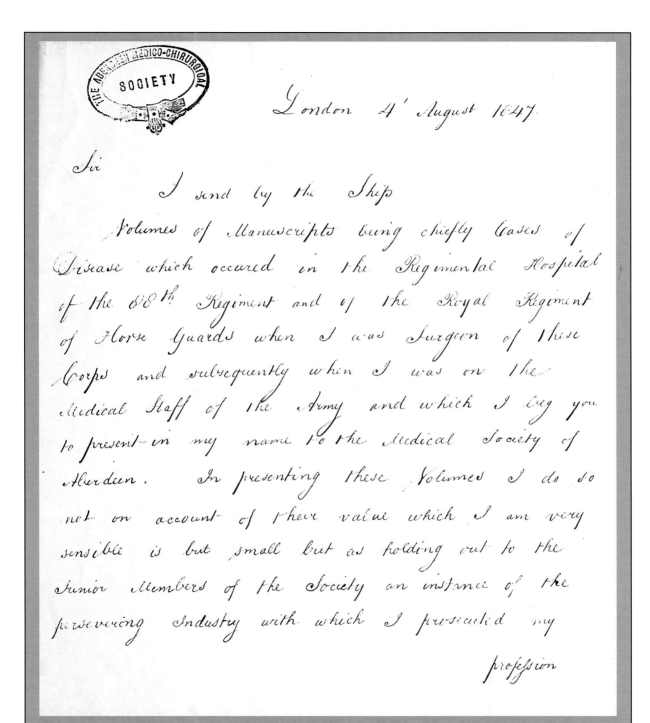

London 4' August 1847.

Sir

I send by the Ship

Volumes of Manuscripts being chiefly Cases of Disease which occured in the Regimental Hospital of the 88th Regiment and of the Royal Regiment of Horse Guards when I was Surgeon of these Corps and subsequently when I was on the Medical Staff of the Army and which I beg you to present in my name to the Medical Society of Aberdeen. In presenting these Volumes I do so not on account of their value which I am very sensible is but small but as holding out to the Junior Members of the Society an instance of the persevering Industry with which I prosecuted my profession

Sir James McGrigor's letter (1847)

The Royal Letters and Telegrams

Three weeks after the outbreak of the 1914-18 war, Prince Albert, later King George VI, developed appendicitis. Sir James Reid, physician to the King in Scotland, received a telegram from Sir Frederick Treves requesting he go to Wick to bring Prince Albert to Aberdeen. This he did on board the hospital ship *'Rohilla'*. On the 9th September 1914, Prince Albert had his appendix removed by Sir John Marnoch, Professor of Surgery at Aberdeen.

There are three letters in King George V's own handwriting, four telegrams, and also a collection of letters and reports by Sir James Reid, Professor Ogston, Sir John Marnoch and Sir Frederick Treves. This collection was gifted to the Society by John Marnoch's daughter, Mrs Cleghorn.

Telegram from King George V
to Sir James Reid (1914)

Letter from King George V
to Sir James Reid (1914)

Joseph Black's Book on the Discovery of Carbon Dioxide (1782)

This valuable little book, published in 1782, is entitled *"Experiments upon magnesia alba, quick-lime, and other alcaline substances; by Joseph Black, MD, Professor of Chemistry in the University of Edinburgh"*. These experiments, which record the discovery of carbon dioxide, are regarded by historians as the origin of the modern science of chemistry.

Professor Black's book (1782)

Dr Kilgour's Letter (1860)

In 1860, the date of the letter, patients were admitted to the Royal Infirmary on recommendation. Very frequently this recommendation was given by the local minister, rather than by a practising doctor. The letter was presented to the Society by the grandson of Mr Watt the Minister of Strathdon, Dr William Todd.

Transcript of Dr Kilgour's letter:

Aberdeen
30th July 1860

My Dear Parson,

Don`t for any sake send any more of your "parishioners" to me with notes of introduction. They don`t pay. Country people when they get a note from their minister make it serve in a genteel sort of a way the purpose of an Infirmary Recommendation - that is to say, they call at our houses and think they are entitled to our advice there on the same terms as at the Infirmary. We are up to the dodge from experience. Your three parishioners acted on the principle. Give them Infirmary Recommendations or Nothing. And if they are too fine to go there, they then know that they have no right to trouble us at our own houses.

I`ll tell you an anecdote of a Strathdon man. Your predecessor some years ago gave an Infirmary line in the usual form to a parishioner who applied on his coming to Aberdeen at the Hospital. It was my day to admit. I could not see anything the matter with him, but as we are always ready to admit persons from a distance I took him in thinking as country people cannot always explain themselves readily a day or two might enable us to find out his complaint.

On the following day he asked to leave to get out for a few minutes which was granted. Some medicine had been ordered which he did not take and on the next day he said to me "ye may sign my ticket (his dismissal) noo, for I have settled my bit business wi Duncan Davidson and I`m gaun hame noo". The rascal was taking bed and board whilst he settled matters in Aberdeen.

Believe me,
Always sincerely yours,
Alex. Kilgour.

Aberdeen
30 July 1860

My Dear Parson,

I went for any sake send any more of your "Parishioners" to me with notes of introduction. They don't pay. Country people when they get a note from their Minister make it serve in a genteel sort of a way the purpose of an Infirmary Recommendation — that is to say, they call at our own houses & think they are entitled to our advice

Dr Kilgour's letter (1860)

The Apprenticeship Agreement (1776)

The apprenticeship agreement, dated 1776, records the contract between Dr William Chalmers, physician in Aberdeen, and William Ross.

The
Apprenticeship
Agreement
(1776)

Transcript of the Apprenticeship Agreement:

AT Aberdeen the eight day of April, one thousand seven hundred and seventy six. It is agreed betwixt Dr Willm Chalmers Physician in Aberdeen on the one part & William Ross lawful son to John Ross Weaver in Old Aberdeen, with the special advice & consent of the said father, on the other part; In manner following, that is to say, the said William Ross with consent foresaid hath bound & engaged & by these presents binds & engages himself as a servant and apprentice to ye said Dr William Chalmers in his business & employment of Physician & Surgeon & that for the space of five full & compleat years from this date. During which space the said William Ross as Principal & for & with him the said John Ross his father as cautioner & surety bind & oblige themselves conjunctly & separately their Heirs, Executors & Successors, that ye said William Ross shall faithfully & honestly serve & obey ye said Dr William Chalmers his Master in the capacity of a house servant & apprentice. That he shall regularly attend & no way absent himself from his said masters service without leave first asked & given under ye penalty of serving two days at ye expiry of this Indenture; or/in his said Masters option of paying to him one shilling sterling for each days absence. That he shall do all ye business of an ordinary common servant ------and without doors, shall take care of-----and attend him wherever he goes. That he shall not conceal from his said Master anything tending to his prejudice but timeously & honestly advertise him thereof. That he shall not upon any pretence whatever reveal or communicate to any person the smallest article of his Masters business of which he may have access to know; That he shall abstain from all kinds of gaming, debauchery & bad company & in general shall behave himself decently & properly in every way as becomes a servant, Apprentice & Citizen. As also the said John Ross as father to ye said William Ross binds & obliges himself to provide ye said William Ross his son in shirts, stockings & washing; And on the other hand the said Dr William Chalmers agrees to dispense with ye payment of ye usual sum of three hundred merks in name of Apprentice for with the said William Ross, & likewise obliges himself to provide & maintain him in board & lodging; and moreover to allow him all necessary cloaths except such as have been already mentioned. And also binds & obliges himself to teach & instruct in him in all & everything relating to his business & employment aforesaid, that he himself knows or his said servant & apprentice is capable to conceive. Lastly both the said parties bind & oblige themselves & their aforesaids to implement & perform ye premises to one another under ye penalty of Ten Pounds sterling to be paid by ye party failing to ye party performing or willing, over & above performance. And for ye more security they consent to the registration hereof in the Book of Council & Session or in any other competent registers - That letters of horning on six days charge & all other execution may pass therein in form & to that effect they constitute.

In witness thereof (written upon stamped paper by Alexander Chalmers Apprentice to the said William Chalmers) the said parties have subscribed these presents- Place, day, month & year of God above written.

Before witnesses, viz. Geo. Gordon lawful son to Robert Gordon of Logie & Alexander Chalmers apprentice to ye said Dr William.

    George Gordon   *Witness William Chalmers*
    Alex Chalmers   *Witness William Ross*
                      John Ross

The Midwifery Certificate (1842)

Our Society established a register of midwives in 1827; it was not until 1915 that the official national register was introduced.

Members of the Society were not allowed to employ unregistered midwives.

The Midwifery Certificate is dated 1842.

Topics covered in the examination for registration included:
- *Anatomy and dimensions of the pelvis*
- *Diseases incidental to pregnancy*
- *Management of labour*
- *Management of children and their common complaints.*

Transcript of the Midwifery Certificate:

Aberdeen 12 July 1842

These are to certify that the bearer thereof *Mrs Isobel Sim*-----has attended *one* course of my Lectures on Midwifery including the treatment of Children and Lying-in Women, and that after repeated examinations, and after having conducted the practical deportment------ to my satisfaction, I do find her and conscientiously believe her to be *fully*----qualified to practice in the capacity of a Midwife, and hereby recommend her to the Employment of the Public at large in whatever place Providence may order her to do.

Alex. Fraser   Senior Surgeon
To the Aberdeen General Dispry.
& Lying-in Institution and
Lecturer in Midwifery in
the Universities of Aberdeen.

N.B. The above testimonial is only granted to those Pupils who are found qualified for the duties of a Midwife. In cases when a certificate is not afforded the Pupil is invited to attend a Second Course of Lectures gratis, or will have her fee returned.

Alexr. Fraser

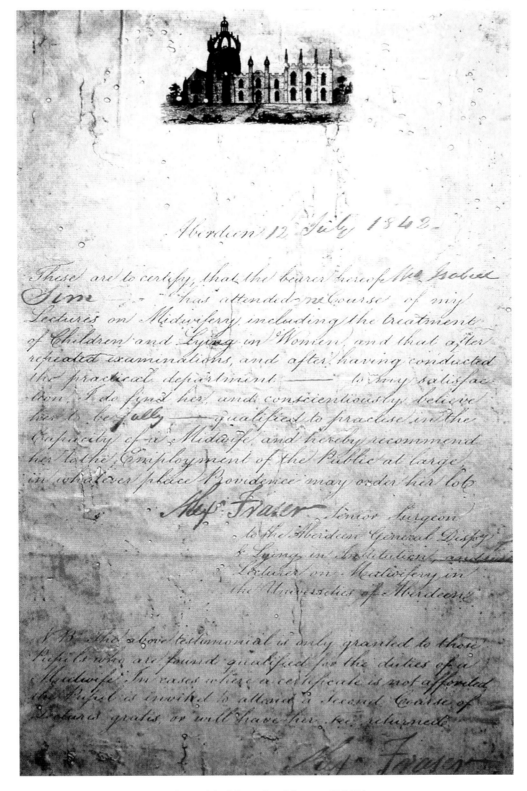

The Midwifery Certificate (1842)

Set of Surgical Instruments

This set of instruments was the property of a country general practitioner and shows the extent of surgery performed by GPs over a hundred years ago. It consists of large amputation knives, a tourniquet and trephine, and has obviously been well used. At that time, major surgery was performed by GPs in the age described as that of *"kitchen table surgery"*.

For example, in the 1840s, Dr Francis Adams of Banchory carried out a mid-thigh amputation of a gangrenous leg in a gamekeeper. The patient made an excellent recovery, was fitted with an artificial limb and was able to resume his activities. An account of the operation was published in 1842.

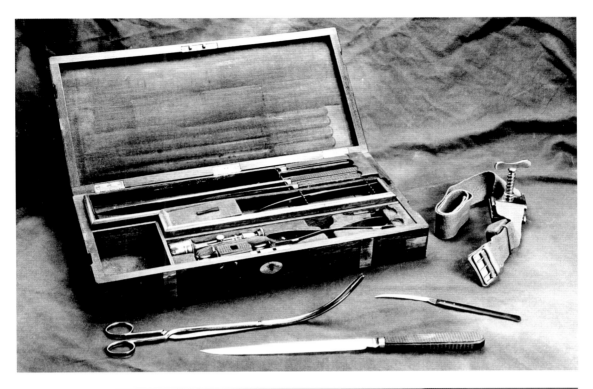

Set of Surgical Instruments

The Collection of Stethoscopes

The Collection of Stethoscopes shows wooden instruments of different shapes and sizes. The oldest has a solid stem. The more recent have hollow stems. The shortest stethoscope is said to be of a size that could be carried under a top hat and the longest is said to be two inches more than the height a flea can jump.

The stethoscope was introduced to Britain by Sir John Forbes (1787-1861). The son of a Banffshire farmer, he attended Aberdeen Grammar School and Marischal College and served an apprenticeship with two Banff Physicians. He practised in the south of England and specialised in chest diseases. In 1821, he published *"A Treatise on the Diseases of the Chest. Translated by John Forbes MD from the latest French edition, De L'Auscultation Médiate by R T H Laënnec, MD"*. This was a translation of the original description of the stethoscope with a commentary by Forbes. By 1840, he had become famous for his expertise in chest diseases and was invited to settle in London where he was appointed one of the first two consultant physicians to the Brompton Hospital for Consumption and Diseases of the Chest. He was elected FRS in 1829 and FRCP in 1849. He was knighted in 1853.

A copy of Forbes' book is in the library.

The Collection of Stethoscopes

The Resuscitation Set

This interesting exhibit dates from 1798. At that time, there was a belief that a vital principle lingered in the intestine after respiration had stopped, and it was thought that by stimulating this vital principle the patient's recovery could be accomplished. The instrument consists of a combustion box with two tubes, one from either side of the box, and a bellows. Tobacco was lit in the box, one tube was inserted into the subject's rectum and the other was attached to the bellows; tobacco smoke was then blown into the intestinal canal for as long as two hours if necessary. These instruments were issued to lock-keepers throughout the country.

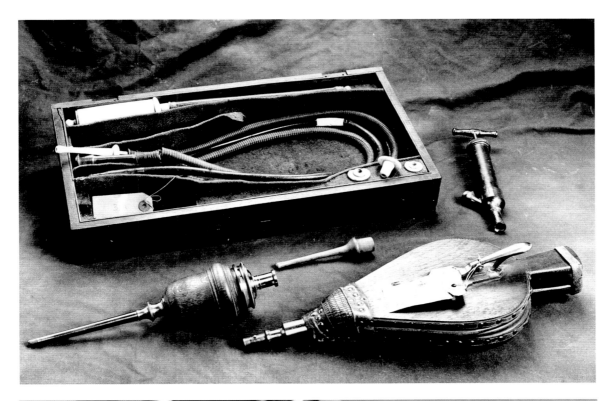

The Resuscitation Set

The Bleeding and Cupping Set

This also dates from 1798. It consists of an instrument known as a scarificator, several cups and a brass syringe. The scarificator was a spring-loaded, multi-bladed instrument which was used to plunge into the patient's flesh to cause bleeding. The desired amount of blood could then be extracted by the use of the cups and, if necessary, also by the syringe.

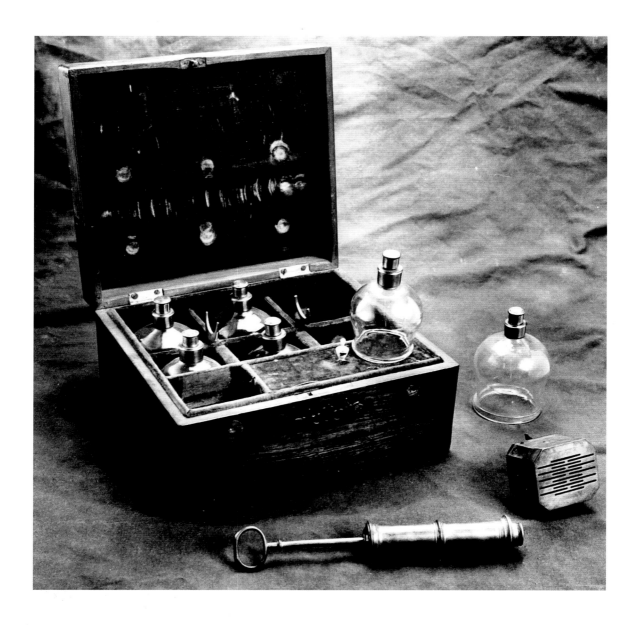

The Bleeding and Cupping Set

Tray of Chinese Instruments

This set of instruments, consisting of acupuncture needles and instruments for operating on the eye, was brought to Aberdeen by a missionary at the time of the Boxer Rising in 1900.

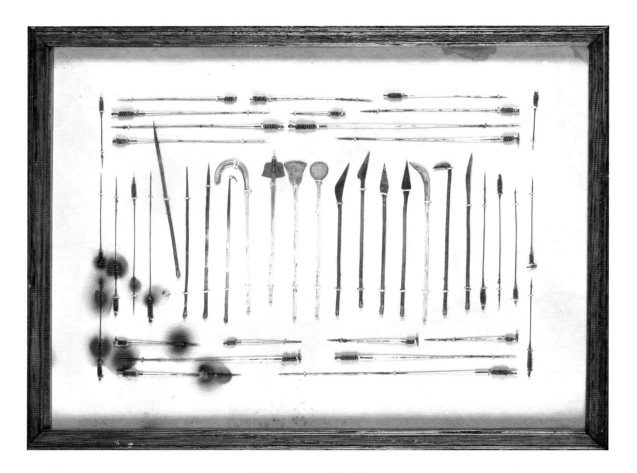

Tray of Chinese surgical instruments

Box of Surgical Instruments

This large box set of surgical instruments, from the Department of Surgery at the University, consists of three stacked trays. It includes a tourniquet and large bone instruments such as saws.

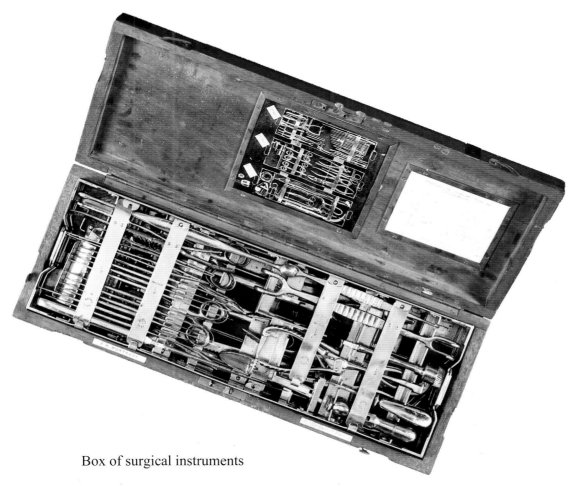

Box of surgical instruments

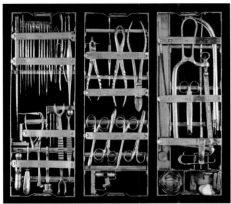

The Society and the Medical School

At the instigation of Bishop Elphinstone of Aberdeen, King James IV wrote to Pope Alexander VI. The result was the Papal Bull of 1495 which contained the following passage: *"We would vouchsafe, ..., to appoint and ordain that there be henceforth and in all times to come a university in the said city of Old Aberdeen, and that a university of general study as well as in theology, canon and civil law, <u>medicine</u> and the liberal arts"*. The first Professor of Medicine (known as the *Mediciner*) was James Cumyne (1503-1522).

Bishop Elphinstone

The Medical School is, therefore, the oldest in the British Isles (and indeed, the English-speaking world), followed by Cambridge in 1540 and Oxford in 1546. St Andrews University was founded in 1411, but there was little evidence of the teaching of medicine; the first recorded appointments in medicine were in 1539.

Over the centuries, the standard of teaching varied. In the 1630's, the standard was high but fell victim to the Civil Wars. When the Society was founded in 1789, teaching was virtually non-existent and, as well as teaching themselves, the members campaigned for the setting up of a medical school. Among the Senior Members whom they lobbied were the professors and lecturers of the university, and these they attacked vigorously in student publications as well as in letters to the senior members. On one occasion, the Junior Members actually wrote suggesting the establishment of an extra-mural medical school; their seniors did not reply. Their efforts bore fruit: lecturers were appointed at Marischal College, and in 1839 Regius Professors of Anatomy and Surgery. There was rivalry between King's and Marischal Colleges: King's styled itself the University of Aberdeen, and referred to the upstart, but young and vigorous rival, as *"... the Broad Street Academy"*. But while Marischal College received increasing support and endowment, and grew in favour as a medical school, King's gradually declined on its medical side, burdened by two successive *Mediciners* (the Bannermans, father and son) who held the Chair of Medicine for 45 years and steadfastly refused to give any lectures.

As well as having two Universities, Aberdeen could also boast of having two medical journals – the Aberdeen Lancet and the Aberdeen Medical Journal. The former, a student publication, was founded for the express purpose of *"scarifying and bleeding"* the teachers in the Medical School to do better. Some of the lecturers are described as being *"lethargic and others ... of a plethoric appearance"*. In the second number (June,

1831), the Editors claim *"to have struck terror and dismay into all the incapables and incurables among our Lecturers and Professors, and to have inspired with some degree of life and activity such as are not diseased beyond all hope of recovery."* There was also opposition elsewhere: the (London) Lancet recorded in 1834 that *"considerable difference of opinion, it appears, exists between "New" and "Old" Aberdeen ... but all agree that the Faculty of Medicine would be better managed in Edinburgh, London, or some large town where facilities of hospitals, medical schools, etc. exist so much superior to those in the small towns of the far north."*

Full development of the school had to await the union of King's and Marischal to become the University of Aberdeen in 1860. Professors were then appointed who became leaders in their fields, and the school became a centre of unrivalled excellence. The *raison d'être* of the Junior Section had by then ceased to exist and it faded away in 1864 to be replaced by the University Medical Society.

Extract from the *Aberdeen Lancet* – a Student's journal (1831)

"It has been our object in our former articles on the Medical School of this place to point out the existing abuses in that Institution, and we propose in our present observations to speak of those remedies which are necessary for the cure of the evils of which we complain. Before proceeding, however, to the ratio medendi, *it will be necessary to recapitulate shortly a little of what we have advanced in our former numbers respecting the defects of the present system of the medical instruction in the Universities of Aberdeen. We have said then that the Professor of Physic in the Marischal College, for whose talents and acquirements we entertain the highest respect has always since his first connexion with the University neglected his duty as a teacher, and acted with partiality in his capacity of chief or dictator of the School. – We have shewn that while he lectured on Anatomy, the interests of the students were considered but as secondary to the other objects he had in view; and though he has done more as a professor than he was wont to do as a lecturer, yet that he has never since his appointment given one complete course of the practice of physic even to the favoured few whom he has been pleased to admit to his library."*

Copy of article from the *Shrewsbury Gazette* (1888)

"Clerius, writing to the Shrewsbury News of 29th Dec. (1888) says: 'Not a few educationalists all over the country are constantly being asked by parents as to the most suitable and desirable of all the medical schools where their sons can be efficiently and suitably equipped for their future profession. There can be little doubt that among them all none can surpass the University of Aberdeen. The writer has no interest whatsoever in singling out this institution save its own intrinsic merits. In the first place, the city is not unduly large, nor are the professors' classes, as in Edinburgh and Glasgow, unduly crowded, to the great detriment of the embryo surgeon or physician. The occupants of the various chairs in this Northern seat of learning are able to give more time and attention to their students, both publicly and privately, than could be expected elsewhere. There is, moreover, the great advantage, at the close of the curriculum, of becoming the possessor of a very respectable degree. It would appear, too, that there are no less than eleven chairs in the medical faculty. One great feature in this Northern seat of learning is the comparative freedom from many of those temptations besetting young men in larger places. These are sometimes formidable.'"

The Annual Founders' Dinner

The first recorded "Annual Supper" took place in 1801. The first dinner to have been held in the Society's King Street Hall was in 1838 to commemorate the 50th year of the Society's existence. Various dignitaries were present, and the company dined at 5 p.m., and *"glee-singers were present ... at a cost of 25/- and liquid refreshments"*!

In 1859, the British Medical Association came to Aberdeen, and the Society entertained them on 20th September. *"40 guests and 20 members breakfasted at 8 a.m., and thereafter wined."*

Again, on 11th September, 1885, the BMA returned and the company breakfasted at 9.00 a.m. Professor John Struthers was in the chair, and he provided champagne for over 100 members and guests.

Up until 1902, it was the duty of the President of the Society to provide champagne for all members and guests at the Annual Dinner. The bills for the dinners and drinks from the 1898 dinner reproduced here show that 20 bottles of champagne were consumed by 43 diners, along with wine, port and spirits. J Scott Riddell, writing in 1922 and having been President the previous year, remarked that this custom, with *"the increase in the membership of the Society, and in the price of champagne, is not likely to be revived."*

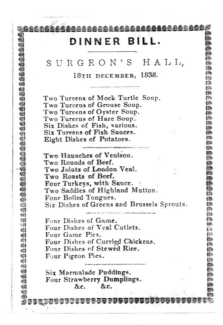

Bill for Annual Founders' Dinner (1838)

Front cover of the programme for the Centenary Founders' Dinner (1889)

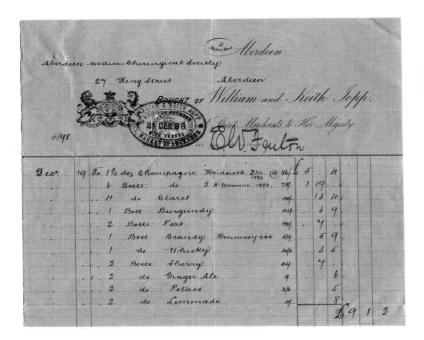

Drinks bill for Annual
Founders' Dinner
(1898)

Dinner bill for Annual
Founders' Dinner
(1898)

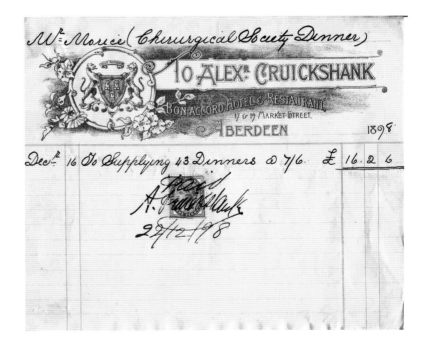

The Minute Books make occasional reference to the Annual Founders' Dinners, such as this extract relating to the 1902 dinner:

> *As one of the members of the Society refused to pay his subscription on account of damage done to his clothes by the chair supplied by the purveyor it was resolved to pay the purveyor the dinner subscriptions minus the one referred to.*

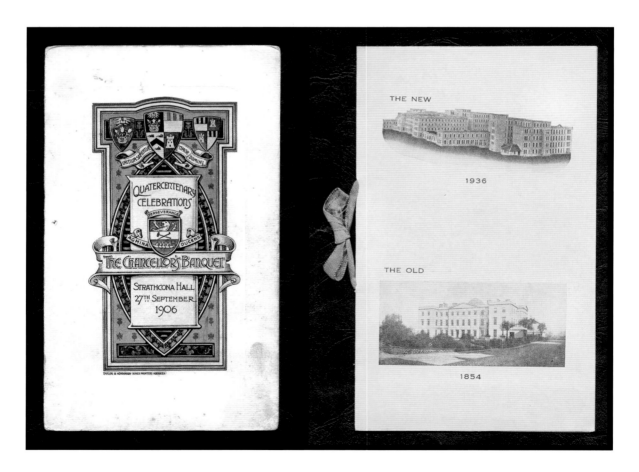

Front covers of the programmes for the Annual Founders' Dinners (1906 & 1936)

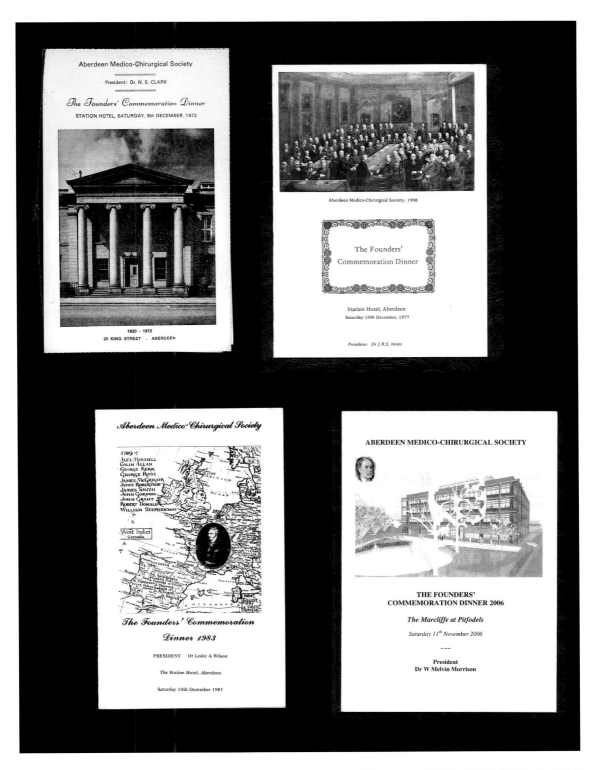

Front covers of the programmes for the Annual Founders' Dinners (1972, 1977, 1983 & 2006)

The Naughton Dunn Fund

Naughton Dunn, MB ChB (1884-1939)

Naughton Dunn was the son of John Dunn, the owner of a shoe shop in Union Street in Aberdeen. He was educated at Aberdeen Grammar School and Aberdeen University. His first post after qualifying was in Scarborough, where he came under the influence of Robert Jones and was taken on as his assistant in Liverpool. Aged 29, he was appointed as the first Orthopaedic Surgeon in Birmingham and spent the rest of his life there, developing a wide-ranging orthopaedic service of outstanding excellence.

He is remembered to-day by the Naughton Dunn Club, the Naughton Dunn Lecture and our own Naughton Dunn Fund.

In his will in 1969, Herbert Shorthouse made a bequest in favour of the Medico-Chirurgical Society, in memory of Naughton Dunn, to show gratitude to a surgeon born and educated in Aberdeen. The fund, known as the *"Naughton Dunn Memorial Trust"*, is administered by the Society for the benefit of "sick, disabled, aged or retired doctors and their widows, priority to be given to those who practise or have practised in the City or County of Aberdeen". Its funds have been carefully managed and it remains healthy – a comforting thought for the current members of the Society.

The Widow's Fund Chest

The formation of the British Orthopaedic Association (1918)
(Naughton Dunn is on the extreme right)

Sir Alexander Ogston was made an Honorary Fellow of the BOA at its inception, one of only three surgeons to be recognised in this way.

First meeting of the British Orthopaedic Association held at Roehampton House, 3 February, 1918. Sitting from left to right: Colonel T. H. Openshaw; Mr E. Muirhead Little; Captain W. E. Bennett. Standing: Major R. B. Osgood; Captain T. P. McMurray; Mr A. S. B. Bankart; Captain D. McCrae Aitken; Captain H. Platt; Major R. C. Elmslie; Mr E. Laming Evans; Captain Naughton Dunn. At the back: Mr W. H. Trethowan and Captain W. R. Bristow. Ranks were those held at the time.

Naughton Dunn (1884-1939)

MISSING TREASURES

After the Union of 1860, aspiring Scottish medical scientists went to the flourishing experimental laboratories in Europe to further their education, and returned to set up research facilities at home. These were the individuals who established Aberdeen as a pre-eminent Medical School. Professors Matthew Hay, Sir Alexander Ogston and Sir John Struthers have been described with their portraits, but others, equally deserving, have no memorial in our Society. These are our *"missing treasures"*.

William Stephenson, MD (1837-1919)

(President of the Medico-Chirurgical Society, 1894-95)

William Stephenson, an Edinburgh graduate, was Professor of Midwifery from 1875 to 1912, during which time he also acted as paediatrician. Though he produced little original work, he was renowned as a teacher and administrator. For ten years he was Dean of the Faculty of Medicine. It is due to his initiative and persistence that the Aberdeen Children's and Maternity Hospitals were founded.

His portrait hangs in Marischal College.

Professor W Stephenson (1837-1919)

William Stirling, MD, DSc (1851-1932)

William Stirling was Professor of Physiology from 1877 to 1886. An Edinburgh graduate, he had studied with the famous Carl Ludwig in Leipzig and, when appointed at the age of 26, already had a string of scientific publications to his name. He completely modernised his department both for research and teaching, so that when he left, his students wrote in Alma Mater: *"Mr Gladstone's government has two great problems to solve, the Irish difficulty, and it has to appoint a suitable successor to Dr Stirling".*

Professor W Stirling (1851-1932)

40   MODERNISATION OF MEDICAL TEACHING

7   A 'City Silhouette' of Professor Stirling in a characteristic pose in *Bon Accord*, II, 1 January 1881, p 4.

Cartoon of Professor W Stirling

John A MacWilliam, MD, FRS, LLD (1857-1937)

John Alexander MacWilliam, who was born in Inverness-shire, graduated at Aberdeen with highest honours. He studied with Ludwig and Kronecker in Germany before working as assistant to Sharpey in London.

PROFESSOR JOHN ALEXANDER MACWILLIAM, M.D., F.R.S.

Professor J A MacWilliam (1857-1937)

He was a pioneer of scientific cardiology; among his many discoveries were:

1. He established the genesis and control of normal cardiac rhythm from a small area near the great veins.
2. He described ventricular fibrillation in the mammalian heart.
3. He noted that the circulation could be maintained by cardiac massage, and that regular rhythm could be restored by electric shock.
4. He introduced an auscultatory method of measuring blood pressure.
5. He demonstrated that chloroform could cause sudden death by ventricular fibrillation.

Three Aberdeen graduates who came under his influence were:

- Augustus D Waller, who made the first recording of an ECG in humans.

- Arthur R Cushny, who was the first to describe atrial fibrillation in a patient.

- Arthur Keith (the famous anatomist), who, with Flack, discovered the sino-atrial node.

They were, according to Sir John McMichael, *"a unique cardiological quartet from the North East"*.

MacWilliam is possibly Aberdeen's greatest medical scientist. Ahead of his time, his discoveries were not applied until times varying from thirty to seventy years after they were made.

His only memorial is an insignificant gravestone in Allanvale cemetery.

David J Hamilton, MB, FRCS(Ed.), LLD, FRS (1849-1909)

Through the efforts of Professors Struthers and Pirrie, a chair of pathology was established in 1882, funded by Sir Erasmus Wilson, and David James Hamilton was appointed professor; he was the first full-time professor of the subject in the UK and, until he retired in 1908, his occupancy of the chair was marked by sustained brilliance in teaching, research and administration.

His three-volume *"Textbook of Pathology"* was the leading source of information on the subject in the UK for many years. He carried out successful research on the bacteriology of animal diseases and of tuberculosis, and was the first to teach bacteriology. In teaching he excelled. The students in Alma Mater wrote: *"He is always working. When he teaches, it is as if his sole end in life were to teach; when he works, it is not different."*

Halliday Sutherland, an Edinburgh student who came to Aberdeen to work with him wrote: *"When he died his teaching lived, because more of his old pupils were Professors of Pathology throughout the Empire than those of any other school. ... David James Hamilton! You were, and are, the greatest teacher I ever knew".*

Professor D J Hamilton
(1849-1909)

John Theodore Cash, MD, LLD, FRS (1854-1936)

(President of the Medico-Chirurgical Society, 1903-04)

J Theodore Cash was Professor of Materia Medica from 1886 to 1919. Born in Manchester, he graduated in Edinburgh and studied on the continent, spending six months in Ludwig's laboratory in Leipzig. He already had many publications to his name when he was appointed to the chair in Aberdeen.

He was a pioneer of experimental pharmacology. He was renowned for his ingenuity, and dexterity in setting up experiments, many of which he carried out on himself. He published many papers in British, French and German journals.

In his Presidential Address to our Society (1904), he made a plea for the adoption of the decimal system of weights and measures; seventy years later his wish was granted.

His hobby was fishing; a salmon fly bears his name.

THEODAH!

Cartoon of Professor Cash
(from *Reminiscences of a Glorious Year: Aberdeen University Medical Class*, 1908-1913)

Professor J T Cash (1854-1936)

Professor Cash's collection of chemicals (1889)

*(This collection of "alkaloids" was purchased from H.
Trommsdorff, Chemis, Erfurt)*

David Rorie, DSO, MD, DPH (1867-1946)

Dr David Rorie was born in Edinburgh, but received his schooling and early university education in Aberdeen. He subsequently graduated in medicine from Edinburgh and set up practice in a Fife mining district in 1894. He was a strong supporter of First-Aid and taught it to many miners during his time as doctor to a group of collieries. In 1905, he moved to Cults where he spent the rest of his working life.

David Rorie was a man of many talents: doctor, folklorist, poet and song-writer, author and editor, and had a distinguished career in the 1914-18 war. As a Territorial, he was called up in 1914 and served throughout the war, ending, with the rank of Colonel, as Assistant Director of Medical Services of the 51st (Highland) Division. He was twice mentioned in dispatches and was awarded the DSO and the Croix de Chevalier of the Legion d'Honneur.

As a doctor he was popular, *"esteemed alike for his skill as a physician and his warm personal interest in the social life of the district"* (Dr A G Anderson).

He was a pioneer of folk-lore, his interest having been kindled by the traditions and beliefs of the mining community where he first worked; in 1908 he was awarded the degree of MD for his thesis on *"Scottish Folk-Medicine"* and he continued to contribute articles on the subject to various journals.

He was the author of many contributions, medical and non-medical, to magazines and journals, and was editor of the Caledonian Medical Journal. He edited the *"Book of Aberdeen"* for the BMA visit to Aberdeen in 1939 and wrote *"A Medico's Luck in the War"*, a humorous account of his war experiences.

His poems and songs were written for entertainment; they are characterised by humour and light-hearted satire. They were immensely popular and were sung by Scots all over the world. Two poems, written to entertain the troops in the trenches, are in our archives. In 1930, he was appointed Poet Laureate to our Society by the President, Dr Henry Peterkin, and ever since, his most popular song *"The Lum Hat"* has been sung by the assembled company at our annual dinner. As Dr Danny Gordon of Ellon put it, *"His humour and wit were a joy. The qualities of head and heart of David Rorie are abundantly present in his verse and prose."*

Cartoon of Dr David Rorie of Cults

"His small, rotund, beautifully dressed and immaculately coiffured figure was a familiar and welcome sight in the chauffeur-driven large two-seater Humber that eventually displaced his horse and gig."
(I A Olson, in *A Bicentennial History*)

David Rorie in uniform
during the Great War

Dr David Rorie
(1867-1946)

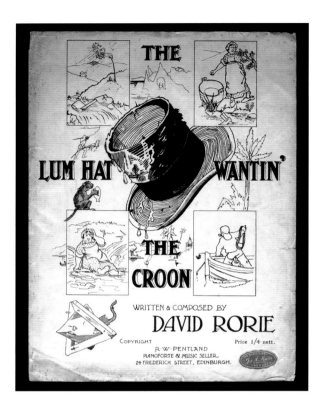

The Lum Hat Wantin' the Croon
Dr David Rorie

The burn was big wi' spate,
An' there cam' tum'lin' doon
Tapsalteerie the half o' a gate,
Wi' an auld fish-hake an' a great muckle skate,
An' a lum hat wantin' the croon!

The auld wife stude on the bank
As they gaed swirlin' roun',
She took a gude look an' syne says she:
"There's food an' there's firin' gaun to the sea,
An' a lum hat wantin' the croon!"

Sae she gruppit the branch o' a saugh,
An' she kickit aff ane o' her shoon,
An' she stuck oot her fit - but it caught in the gate,
An' awa' she went wi' the great muckle skate,
An' the lum hat wantin' the croon!

She floatit fu' mony a mile,
Past cottage an' village an' toon,
She'd an awfu' time astride o' the gate,
Though it seemed to gree fine wi' the great muckle
skate,
An' the lum hat wantin' the croon!

A fisher was walkin' the deck,
By the licht o' his pipe an' the mune,
When he sees an auld body astride o' a gate,
Come bobbin' alang in the waves wi' a skate,
An' a lum hat wantin' the croon!

"There's a man overboord!" cries he,
"Ye leear!" says she, "I'll droon!
A man on a boord! It's a wife on a gate,
It's auld Mistress Mackintosh here wi' a skate,
An' a lum hat wantin' the croon!"

Was she nippit to death at the Pole?
Has India bakit her broon?
I canna tell that, but whatever her fate,
I'll wager ye'll find it was shared by a skate,
An' a lum hat wantin' the croon!

There's a moral attached to my sang,
On greed ye should aye gie a froon,
When ye think o' the wife that was lost for a gate,
An' auld fish-hake an' a great muckle skate,
An' a lum hat wantin' the croon!

In more recent times Aberdeen medical scientists have continued to make discoveries of fundamental importance.

Sir Alastair Currie, BSc, MB(Glas), FRCS(Ed)&(Glas), FRCPath, FRSE (1921-1994)

Sir Alastair was Regius Professor of Pathology in Aberdeen 1962-72 and in Edinburgh 1972-86. He was President of the Royal Society of Edinburgh 1991-93, and was the outstanding research pathologist of his day.

While in Aberdeen, he, with John Kerr and Andrew Wylie, discovered the phenomenon known as programmed cell death which, with the Professor of Greek, he named *"apoptosis"* or *"falling of leaves"*. From 1990 onwards this has caused immense research interest – today Google has over 17 million references to *"apoptosis"*.

Professor Sir Alastair Currie
(1921-1994)

Hans W Kosterlitz, MD, PhD, DSc, FRS (Edin & Lond), FRCPE, LLD (Liege & Dundee) (1903-1996)

(Honorary Member of the Society)

Hans Walker Kosterlitz was born and educated in Berlin, where he graduated MD in 1929. In 1933, he fled from Nazism and in 1934, he joined Professor J J R Macleod in the Department of Physiology in Aberdeen. He was successively Research Worker, Assistant Lecturer, Senior Lecturer and Reader. From 1968 to 1973, he was Professor of Pharmacology and from 1973 to 1995, Director of the Unit for Research on Addictive Drugs. In a lifetime of research he published more than 300 articles.

In 1975, with John Hughes, he was the first to demonstrate that the brain produced endorphins, naturally occurring chemicals with widespread effects, including pain relief. This discovery has revolutionised the understanding of how drugs affect the brain, provided an insight into why people become addicted to drugs and has instituted a whole new field of research.

Professor Hans W Kosterlitz (1903-1996)

John R Mallard, OBE, PhD, DSc, FRS(Ed) (1927-   )

(Honorary Member of the Society)

John Rowland Mallard was appointed to the Chair of Medical Physics in 1965, the first such chair in Scotland. From small beginnings until his retiral in 1992, he built up a highly successful department where many discoveries and advances in medical imaging were made. In recognition of these, Aberdeen University was awarded the Queen's Anniversary Prize for Higher and Further Education in 2001.

Building on the work of Lauterbur, he and his team made a major breakthrough in the development of Magnetic Resonance Imaging (MRI) when they discovered a technique known as "spin warp" which produced images not spoilt by patient movement – a method used in all MRI scanners to this day. Using this technique, the team produced, in 1980, a whole body MRI scan, a world first.

Professor Mallard received many honours and prizes, including the gold medal of the Royal Society of Edinburgh and the Freedom of the City of Aberdeen. He received honorary degrees from the Universities of Hull, Nottingham and Aberdeen.

The first whole body
MRI scanner

Professor John R Mallard (1927-   )

Endpiece

In 1990, on the 250th anniversary of the foundation of Aberdeen Royal Infirmary, Her Royal Highness, Queen Elizabeth the Queen Mother, sent a letter of congratulations. She had a long association with the hospital, as she had accompanied her husband, the Duke of York (later King George VI), when he officially opened the new Infirmary in 1936, marking the achievement of the vision of Matthew Hay, Ashley Mackintosh and Andrew Lewis.

HRH Queen Elizabeth, the Queen Mother

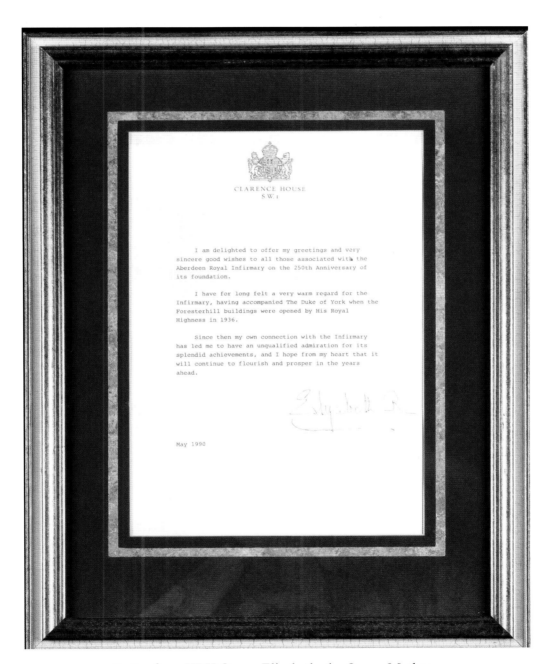

Letter from HRH Queen Elizabeth, the Queen Mother

INDEX

Aberdeen Infirmary *57*
Aberdeen Lancet 154, *155*
Aberdeen Medical Journal 154
Aberdeen Medical Women's Federation 107
Aberdeen Medico-Chirurgical Society 14, 94-96, **154**
Aberdeen Royal Infirmary at Foresterhill *57*
Aberdeen Royal Infirmary at Woolmanhill *49, 57*
Aberdeen Town Council Minutes (1641) *19*
Adam Quaich *133*
Adams, Andrew Leith 76
Adams, Francis *75*, **76**, *76-7*, 144
Albert, Prince, later King George V1 136
Allan, Colin **14**, 15
Anatomical Drawings of Alberto Morrocco **86**, *87*
Anatomy 40, 72, 84, 86
Anatomy: Lockhart, Hamilton and Fyfe – *The Anatomy of the Human Body* 72, 86
Anderson Gold Medal 102
Anderson, Andrew 30
Anderson, James 102
Anderson, Sir Alexander Greig **68**, *69*, 83, 168
Antisepsis 44
Apoptosis 171
Appendicectomy on Price Albert 60, 136
Appleby, Malcolm 96
Apprenticeship Agreement **140**, *140*
Archives, McGrigor **134**
Army Medical Services 2, *111*
Baird, David 78
Baird, Sir Dugald **70**, *70-1*
Bajan of the University of Aberdeen *46*
Ballot Boxes **110**, *110*
Banchory 10, 76
Bannerman, Professors 154
Bell, Clifford Thiselton 112, *113*
Bill for Annual Founder's Dinner *157*
Bishop Elphinstone 154, *154*
Black, Joseph: Book 137
Bladder Stones *103*
Blaikie, Patrick 91
Bleeding and Cupping Set **150**, *151*
Bliss, Michael 52
Body-snatching 10, 84
Bowie, Harold 50, 52
Bowie, Violet 50, 52
Box of Surgical Instruments *153*
British Medical Association 156
British Medical Journal 44

British Orthopaedic Association 160
Brodie, William **76**
Burgess, Free, of Guild 18
Bursaries, Med-Chi Student Elective 133
Byron, Lord 20, *20*
Candlesticks, Silver **99**, *99*
Cantlie, Sir James 50, 104, 105
Carbon Dioxide, Book on the Discovery of **137**, *137*
Cash, John Theodore 64, **166**, *166*
Cash, Professor: Collection of Chemicals *167*
CBE, Dr Mary Esslemont's **106**, *106*
Centenary Founders' Dinner 156
Certificate, Junior Member's **132**, *132*
Certificate, Strachan Bursary *133*
Certification of Midwives 28, **142**, *143*
Chair, Junior Members' President's **123**, *123*
Chair, Presidential **121**, *121*
Chairs, Members' **122**, *122*
Chalmers Cartoon **89***, 89*
Chalmers, William 89, 140-1
Chemical collection of Professor Cash *167*
Chinese Instruments **152**, *152*
Christie, J F 108
Cigarette Card Album - *First Aid* **105**, *105*
Cleghorn, Mrs 136
Collection of Stethoscopes **146**, *147*
Council Chamber in the Med-Chi *119*
Craig, John 80
Crawford, Robert Cree **62**
Crocodile 40, *43*
Cromar, Cuthbert Alexander 112, *113*
Cumming, Ronnie 44
Cumyne, James 154
Currie, Professor Sir Alastair **171**, *171*
Cushny, Arthur R 164
Darwin, Charles 40
Davidson, George 54
Dinner, Annual Founders' **156**-59
Dinner, Centenary Founders' 156
Dissection, The Painting of a **84**, *85*
Donald (Harvey), Robert **8**, *9,* 14, 15
Dunn, Naughton **160**, *161*
Dyce, Robert 28
Dyce, William (artist) 1, 28, 43
Dyce, William (physician) **28**, *29*
Eenoolooapik 124, *125*
Elective Bursaries, Med-Chi Student 133
Elephantiasis 50
Elphinstone, Bishop 154, *154*

Emblem of the Society iii
Engraved plate of the Society **94**, *94*
Esslemont, Dr Mary **106**, *106*, 107
Farquhar, Sir Walter 16
Finlay, Professor David W **62**, *63*, 64
First-Aid 104, 105, 168
First-Aid book *104*
Forbes, Alastair, 120
Forbes, Sir John 146
Fordyce, Sir William 22
Foresterhill Building **117**, *117*
Foresterhill, Aberdeen Royal Infirmary *57*
Founders' Dinner, Annual **156**-59
Founders' Dinner, Centenary 156
Founders' Plaque **14**, *15*
Fraser, Alexander 142
Free Burgess of Guild 18
Freedom of the City of Aberdeen 16, 70, 106, 173
French, George **22**, *23*
Gambly, Henry Snell 83
Geddes, Andrew 1, **4**
George V, King 136
Giles, James 1, **12**, 30, 32, 34, 36, 38, 84
Golf Cup, The Ashley Mackintosh **98**, *98*
Gordon, Alexander – *Treatise on the Epidemic Puerperal Fever; Plaque* 8, 28
Gordon, Danny 168
Gordon, John 14, 15
Gown, Presidential **97**, *97*
Grandfather Clock **108**, *108*
Grant, John **6**, *7*, 14, 15, 128
Gray, Sir Henry 54
Gunn, Sir James 72
Hall in the Med-Chi *118*
Hamewith and Other Poems 83
Hamilton, Professor David J 60, **165**, *165*
Harvey, Albert 8
Harvey, Alexander 8, **80**, *81*
Harvey, Robert **8**, *9*, 14, 80
Harvey, William 10, **16**-19, *17*
Hay, Matthew: Cartoon iv
Hay, Professor Matthew v, **54**-7, *54-6*, 58, 64
Hippocrates 76, 95, 120
Hippocrates, The Etching of **90**, *90*
Hogarth Cartoon **88**, *88*
Hong Kong 50
Howie, Sir James 72
HRH Queen Elizabeth, the Queen Mother **174**-5
Hughes, John 172
Hutcheon David **32**, *32, 33*
Instruments, Box of Surgical **153**, *153*
Instruments, Set of Surgical **144**, *145*
Instruments, Tray of Chinese **152**, *152*

Insulin 52
James IV, King 154
Jamesone, George 1
Jamieson, Robert **26**, *27*
Johnston, John 60, 109
Joint Hospitals Scheme at Foresterhill v, 54, 58
Jones, Robert 160
Junior Member's Certificate **132**, *132*
Junior Members' President's Chair **123**, *123*
Kai Ho, Kai 50
Kayak **124**-5
Keith Gold Medal **103**, *103*
Keith, Major George 103
Keith, Sir Arthur 40, 164
Keith, William 103
Kellas, Arthur 112, *113*
Kelly, William 112
Kerr, George **10**, *11*, 14, 15
Kerr, John 171
Kilgour, Alexander **78**, *79*
Kilgour's letter (1860) **138**-9
King George V 136
King James IV 154
King Street Hall **114**, *114-5*
King's College 154
Kosterlitz, Hans W 133, **172**, *172*
Laing, Rev. William **38**, *39*
Lancet 155
Lectern **109**, *109*
Library 6, **126**, *126*
Library in the King Street Hall 138
Lister, Arthur Hugh 64, 112, *113*
Lister, Lord 44, 78, 112
Livingston, William **20**, *21*, 22
Lockhart, Mrs Elizabeth 72, *74*
Lockhart, Professor R D **72**-4, *73, 74*, 86
London School of Tropical Medicine 50
Lum Hat, The 168, *170*
Lumsden, Harry Leith 123
MacKay, Joseph 14, 15
Mackintosh, Edith 58
Mackintosh, Professor Sir Ashley v, 54, 56, **58**, *59*, 64, 83, 97, 98, 133, 174
Macleod, Professor John J R **52**, *52, 53*, 172
Macleod, Professor: Nobel Prize Medal *52*
MacWilliam, John A 64, **164**, *164*
Magnetic Resonance Imaging 173
Malaria 50
Mallard, John R 133, **173**, *173*
Manson, Professor Sir Patrick **50**, *51*, 133
Marischal College 5, 154
Marnoch, Sir John 60, *61*, 64, 136
McGrigor Archives **134**

McGrigor Centenary Plaque **111**, *111*
McGrigor, Jamie MSP *4*
McGrigor, Sir James **2**-5, *3*, 14, 15, *75*, **82**, *82*, 84, 114, 116, 121, 129, 133
McGrigor's Obelisk *5*
Medallion, Presidential **96**, *96, 97*
Med-Chi Student Elective Bursaries and the Adam Quaich 133
Medical School 154-5
Medical School: Hong Kong, Chinese 50
Medical Society 2, 4, 84, 154-5
Medical Women's Federation Medallion **107**, *107*
Medico-Chirurgical Society members in 1908 **64**, *65*
Medico-Chirurgical Society of Aberdeen v, 14, *15*, 20, 40, 94-7, 154-5
Medico-Chirurgical Society's Hall at Foresterhill **117**-9, *118*
Members' Chairs **122**, *122*
Microscope from Professor Ogston's Dept. *48*
Midletun, Alexander 19
Midwifery 28, 70, 142, 162
Midwifery Certificate 28, **142**, *143*
Milne, G P vi, 82
Milne, Joseph Ellis 112, 113
Minute Books 4, *34*, **128**-31, 140-3, 158
Mitcalff, Adrian 19
Mitchell, Alexander 14, 15
Mitchell, Charles 91, 93
Moir, James **12**, *13*, 14, 15
Moir, John 1, **20**, 22, 24
Monkey contemplating a human skull **100**, *101*
Morningfield Hospital 68, 78
Morrice, Thomas 32
Morrocco, Alberto 1, **70**, 72, 74, 86-7
Mortsafes: Banchory and Skene churchyards 10
MRI scanner *173*
Munro, Neil 83
Murray, Charles **83**, *83*
Napoleon, Bonaparte **91**-3, *91*
Naughton Dunn **160**, *161*
Naughton Dunn Fund **160**
Nichol, Janet C 103
Nicoll, Dr J Patrick S **66**, *67*
Nicolle, Charles 54
Nobel Prize, Professor J J R Macleod's *52*
Noble, James Dickson 112, 113
Obelisk, McGrigor's *5*
Ogilvie, John C **36**, *37*
Ogilvie-Forbes, George 36
Ogston, Professor Sir Alexander **44**-9, *45-7*, 64, 160

Ogston's antiseptic spray *47-8*
Old Mill 30, 112
Olson, I A 168
Osborne, Malcolm 68
Paulus Aegineta, The Seven Books of 76
Peninsular War 2, 134
Penny, Captain 124
Peterhead 38
Peterkin, Henry 58, 168
Phillip, John 1
Pirrie, Professor William **124**, *124*, 165
Plane Tree and Plaque **120**, *120*
Plate of the Society **94**, *94*
Presidential Chair **121**, *121*
Prince Albert, later King George V1 136
Puerperal fever 8, 12
Quaich, The Adam **133**, *133*
Queen Elizabeth, HRH, the Queen Mother **174**-5
Regulations of the Society *130*, 131
Reid, Sir George 1, 26, 40
Reid, Sir James 136
Resurrectionism 10
Resuscitation Set **148**, *149*
Rheinhold, Hugo *'Monkey contemplating a human skull'* **100**, *101*
Rhododendrons: Professor Lockhart 72, *74*
Riddell, J Scott vi, *vi*, 40, 64
Robertson, James (founder) 14, 15, 128, 134
Robertson, James, Lt Col 112-3
Rorie, David 64, 83, 100, **168**-70, *168-9*
Ross, William 140-1
Royal Army Medical College at Millbank 82
Royal Cornhill Hospital 26
Royal Letters and Telegrams 60, **136**, *136*
Scarificator 150, *150-1*
Seal, of the Society **95**, *95*
Set of Surgical Instruments **144**, *145*
Shepherd Memorial Gold Medal **104**
Shepherd, Surgeon Major Peter 104, *104*
Shepherd, William 14, 15
Shorthouse, Herbert 160
Shrewsbury Gazette 155
Silver Candlesticks **99**, *99*
Silver Medal in the Practice of Medicine **102**, *102*
Simms, Charles 56
Simpson, Archibald 2, 114
Smith, James 14, 15
Smith, K M N 66
Souter, John Bulloch 1, **58**, 66
Souter, W Clark 58
Spa, Peterhead 38
Spark, William 108
Spray, Ogston's antiseptic *47-8*

Staphylococcus 44
Stephenson, Professor William 64, **162**, *162*
Stethoscopes, The Collection of **146**, *147*
Stewart (Stuart), John **24**, *25*
Stirling, Professor William **163**, *163*
Strachan Bursary **133**
Strachan, William 133
Struthers, Professor Sir John **40**-3, *41-2*, 156,
Stuart, John **24**, *25*
Student, Med-Chi Elective Bursaries 133
Students' Notes **127**, *127*
Subscription List **116**, *116*
Surgical Instruments, Box of **153**, *153*
Surgical Instruments, Set of **144**, *145*
Todd, William 138
Tray of Chinese instruments **152**, *152*
Treves, Sir Frederick 136
Typhus 54
Waller, Augustus D 164
War Memorial Plaque **112**, *113*
Watchtower in Banchory Churchyard *10*
Watt, George **30**, *31*
Watt, George Fiddes 1, **44**-6, 83
Wellington, The Duke of 2
Whale 40
Whitehead, Joseph 78, **80**
Widows' Fund Chest 160
Williamson, Eliza 34
Williamson, Joseph **34**, *35*
Woodend Hospital 30
Woolmanhill, Aberdeen Royal Infirmary *49, 57*
Wright, Edward M 117
Wylie, Andrew 171